value of the
System

The bidding methods outlined in this book are in complete conformity with the new International Contract Bridge Laws and Scoring, which went into effect on March 31, 1935.

The FOUR ACES SYSTEM *of Contract Bridge*

BY

OSWALD JACOBY   DAVID BURNSTINE

HOWARD SCHENKEN

MICHAEL T. GOTTLIEB

Introduction by
HAROLD S. VANDERBILT

THE FOUR ACES, INC.

NEW YORK

Publishers' Note

"THE Four Aces System of Contract Bridge" is unique among books on Bridge for several reasons.

First, it is the only book ever written by a team of champion Bridge players. Others may claim to be the champions, but the record speaks for itself.* The Four Aces team has been recognized as the leading team of the country every year since its formation.

Second, the book is an accurate description of how these champions bid.

Third, there has been no need to include any pet theories advanced by any individual. The system is a harmonious unit, not a collection of ideas superimposed one upon the other.

Finally, it is not an experimental system—every theory has been tried out against the strongest competition and proven brilliantly successful.

This book, which represents a year and a half of work by the authors, might be said to have been written in three stages. The first or experimental stage was from August 1933 to February 1934, during which time the authors studied their own methods of bidding in order to make possible a simple presentation.

The second stage, from February 1934 to December 1934, was the writing period. The third and most im-

* See p. ix.

portant stage was the period between November 15, 1934 and February 15, 1935, when the material was collated and edited.

The authors and their collaborators have been responsible for practically every constructive innovation in Contract bidding. For instance, going back to the early days of Contract, the Forcing two-bid and the two-notrump response were invented by Waldemar von Zedtwitz, a collaborator of this book, and used by him and others for several months before they were incorporated in any system.

The original and basic features of the Four Aces System include:

1. The Four Aces Valuation Table—the simplest and most accurate valuation basis ever devised.
2. The Principle of Anticipation.
3. The Principle of Risk versus Gain, applied to defensive bidding.
4. The Limiting Theory of notrump bids.
5. The Rule of the Ace and the King in Slam bidding.
6. The Opening bid the same in any position, *irrespective of vulnerability.*
7. The Tactical and Positional bids.
8. The Exploratory response—two of a lower ranking suit.
9. All Jump bids by Responding Hand forcing to game.
10. The Jump Two-Over-One response—forcing to a Slam.
11. The Double of an Opening one notrump for business—not for a Takeout.
12. The Slam Invitational Game Force.

Because these important features are interlocking parts of a unified and complete system, it is impossible for anyone successfully to graft any of them on his own bidding system.

The way to win is to play the Four Aces System in its entirety—from A to Z. The system is extremely simple—expressed in everyday language. It is easily understood and can be learned quickly by anyone, whether a beginner or an experienced player.

THE PUBLISHERS

Championship Record of Leading National Tournaments Since Formation of the Four Aces Team

FOLLOWING is the record of the major tournaments * since the formation of the Four Aces Team, in August, 1933. The Four Aces Team consists of David Burnstine, Oswald Jacoby, Michael T. Gottlieb, and Howard Schenken. As the record below shows, the Four Aces Team, playing their system, have won 11 out of 13 major championship events:

WON BY THE FOUR ACES		WON BY ALL OTHERS**	
August 1933	Asbury Park Trophy (Team-of-Four) of the American Bridge League.		
August 1933	Masters Pair, Asbury Park, American Bridge League (Burnstine and Schenken).	November 1933	Vanderbilt Cup (Team-of-Four) by Frank Rendon, Sydney Rusinow, B. H. Feuer and Philip Abrahamson.

* The December events of the American Bridge League and the 1934 Congress of the American Whist League have been omitted, since the Four Aces Team did not play in them.

** Teams captained by Ely Culbertson and P. Hal Sims participated in many of these events, but neither team reached the finals.

WON BY THE FOUR ACES		WON BY ALL OTHERS	
January 1934	Grand National Trophy (Team-of-Four) of the United States Bridge Association.		
January 1934	Grand National Pair of the United States Bridge Association (Gottlieb and Schenken).		
March 1934	Reisinger Cup (Team-of-Four) of the Eastern Bridge Championships.		
March 1934	Goldman Cup, Eastern Pair Championship (Burnstine and Jacoby).		
August 1934	Masters Pair, Asbury Park, the American Bridge League, (Schenken won permanent possession of the cup).	August 1934	Asbury Park Trophy (Team-of-Four) of the American Bridge League by Foster Hopkins, Charles Porter, Jeff Glick and Aaron Frank.
August 1934	Men's Pair, Asbury Park, American Bridge League (Burnstine and Jacoby).		

WON BY THE FOUR ACES	WON BY ALL OTHERS
September 1934 — Spingold Cup (Team-of-Four) of the American Bridge League, entitling the Four Aces officially to represent the United States in the 1935 International Bridge Contest at Budapest against the Hungarian Team, champions of Europe.	
November 1934 — Vanderbilt Cup (Team-of-Four).	
February 1935 — Grand National Trophy (Team-of-Four) of the United States Bridge Association.***	

*** In the quarter-finals of this event the Four Aces Team defeated and eliminated the team of Ely Culbertson, Josephine Culbertson, Theodore A. Lightner and Albert H. Morehead by 5,380 points. This was a decisive test of the respective merits of the Four Aces System and the Culbertson System, and the result showed an average gain of 135 points for the Four Aces System on each of the same hands played by both teams.

Introduction

By HAROLD S. VANDERBILT

BIDDING at Contract Bridge is an exact science, and in order to get the best results it is necessary for a partnership to follow a well-devised system. Any partnership which disregards systems and bids along what it terms "common-sense" lines is bound to end on the rocks before it has weathered perhaps even a single storm.

The best system at Contract is the one which results in securing the largest percentage of makable games and Slams coupled with suffering the minimum number of sizable penalties. Deception is an indispensable part of any good bidding system, for by its use defensive play is made more difficult and the opportunities to inflict penalties are enhanced. In my opinion, the deceptive feature of the system advocated in this book is one of its strongest assets.

The crucial test of any system is its ability to survive when used in gruelling competition over a period of time. Theories may be beautiful and well devised, but in games, as in life, it is practical results which count. The tournament record of the authors of this book during the past two years is known everywhere. Its supreme excellence is the best index of the value of the system which they have developed and employ. This book contains a careful and conscientious analysis of their winning system, the salient features of which they are disclosing to the Contract world

xiii

for the first time. Some of you readers may take exception to this or that feature and decide to vary it, but I cannot urge you too strongly, if you adopt this system, to play it as a whole. Do not attempt to improve on it, for what you deem an improvement in one direction will probably lead to a half dozen pitfalls in another. Remember that this system is the joint product of several master minds, that all of its parts have been carefully attuned, painstakingly tested and blended into a most comprehensive whole.

In reading the manuscript I have been most favorably impressed by the authors' advocacy of a number of, to the Bridge-playing public, new principles, many of which have been devised to keep the bidding on the lowest possible level, and at the same time permit the maximum exchange of information.

Outstanding features of the system include:

The Principle of Anticipation, i.e., when bidding having in mind partner's most probable response;

An original bid of one in a minor on a three-card suit with certain type holdings—a most valuable bid;

Limiting of the one-notrump response to hands of no-trump pattern;

Low biddable requirements for a suit bid;

Extreme flexibility—the word "never" is conspicuously absent from the text.

I consider this book by far the most valuable of recent contributions to Contract Bridge literature.

Authors' Introduction

IN THIS volume the authors present a complete exposition of the practical theories and methods underlying the Four Aces System of Bidding, rather than a rigid individual system with obvious limitations. Years devoted to analysis, tournament competition and rubber play against strong opposition have convinced us that the conclusions set forth in this book are eminently sound and the best yet devised. And because the keynote of our method is extreme flexibility, the reader will find scope for individual variations and choice of procedure, as distinct from fixed rules which, if adhered to rigidly, often lead to disaster.

Stated simply, the object of Contract Rubber Bridge is to gain the maximum number of points when holding good cards and to lose the minimum when less fortunate. With this aim in view, the player should bear in mind and distinguish between three main considerations:

1. *The Principle of Attack.* Applied to hands with which a partnership strives or purposes to bid for game, Slam or safe partial score with little or no interference from opponents. Soundness, precision, and complete exchange of information are essential in reaching the goal.

2. *The Principle of Defense,* designed to minimize the score which your opponents may make with their good hands. This is accomplished by defensive bidding, which, like attacking bidding, de-

pends primarily on soundness and precision, but
which may occasionally embrace irregular and deceptive bids, made primarily not for the purpose
of conveying information to partner, but rather
to mislead or otherwise embarrass opponents.

3. *The Principle of Safety,* most important of all,
   which cautions the player to avoid rash, ill-timed,
   or dangerous action, and at all times carefully to
   weigh the advantages to be gained by any contemplated course, against possible losses. Mastery
   of safe methods necessarily precedes the acquisi-
   tion of real skill at Contract, just as successful
   warfare depends largely on good equipment.

Safety, attack and defense are the three angles from
which master players judge their hands and which form
the theoretical background and the basis for their solution
of bidding problems. Defense has as its objective, *interference with the enemy,* and should be used in the most
diverse manner compatible with safety, while concerted
attack, once decided upon, proceeds by the use of several
more specific principles, as follows:

1. *The Development or Flow Principle.* This consists
of a slow and logical development of bidding which proceeds in an even flow, rather than in a leaping hit-or-miss
fashion, toward the final declaration.

2. *The Principle of Limits.* In accordance with the Development Principle, any bid made under our system
shows certain limits to the strength of our hand and each
succeeding bid serves more clearly to define these limits,
eventually enabling our partner to visualize a complete
and accurate picture of our holding.

3. *The Forcing Principle.* The study of logical bidding
methods indicates clearly the general impossibility of

showing your entire strength by one bid. It is necessary to
sound out not only what high cards partner holds, but also
his distribution. Accordingly, most bids, in the early stages
of the contracting, are made with the *hope* that our partner will continue the bidding; however, with *certain* bids
we *demand* that partner respond, thus assuring us an opportunity to take further action. These bids are called
Forcing bids. There are two types:

1. *The Game Force* which says, "Partner, we have
game in this hand. We must continue the bidding until a
game bid has been reached." Under our system there are
several such bids, one of which is the Opening bid of two
in a suit.

2. *The Temporary Force,* sometimes called the Exploratory Bid. A Temporary Force merely forces partner
to respond once, and a player making a Temporary Force
may have the intention of passing at his next bid; for instance, when a One-Over-One response is made with a
weak hand.

These two types of bids are known as *Absolute Forces,*
since we not only expect partner to respond, but *know* that
he will.

There is another type of bid in the Four Aces System
known as the *Qualified Force.*

The Qualified Force is made with the expectation that
partner will not pass, but, on very rare occasions, he may
pass when, by the Principle of Limits, he clearly realizes
that there is practically no chance for a game.

Just as there are two types of Absolute Forces, there
are two types of Qualified Forces.

The Qualified Game Force conveys the message, "Partner, I expect but do not absolutely demand that you re-

spond. However, if you do respond, the bidding must continue to game."

The Qualified Temporary Force is an Exploratory bid made by a player who has previously limited the strength of his hand by a pass.

Finally, not only as a principle of attack, but as the fundamental basis of our entire system, we come to the *Principle of Anticipation*. This Principle of Anticipation, as all impartial Bridge experts and writers familiar with championship tournament play know and readily attest, was originated and developed by the Four Aces Team long before some scattered and incomplete ideas regarding this principle were rushed under similar names into print elsewhere. The ability to anticipate and prepare for probable future action of partner and opponents changes a beginner into a fair player, a fair player into a good player, and a good player into a master.

If it is our turn to bid and we decide to make a call, the decision is reached, not because we follow blindly any fixed rigid rule, but rather because we anticipate that it is the best course to follow. Having made the decision, we now select our bid, again not according to rule, but for the purpose of simplifying as much as possible our future course of action. This Principle of Anticipation (which is, in effect, the principle of simplicity) will be emphasized throughout this book. The attention given it is commensurate with its great importance. Remember, that in order to play Contract well you must bid well and in order to bid well you must carefully plan your *future course*.

In this book we introduce the concept that while the Opening bid is made for one or more of several reasons, the great majority of such bids are made as the first step in a concerted attack. Therefore, in undertaking to learn

the Four Aces System the reader will do well to follow
the principle: *The requirements for an Opening bid
should be the same in any position, and whether vulnerable
or not.** Such bids are discussed in Part I.

Without departing from the general principle that any
hand which warrants an Opening bid in first or second
position does so in third or fourth, we recognize that for
tactical or defensive reasons certain hands may be opened
in third or fourth position which should not be opened
in first or second. Such hands occur infrequently. However, as a good player should use such bids from time to
time, they are treated in Part II of this book. There we
also discuss defensive and competitive bidding, and Slam
bidding. While Slam bidding is presented separately, the
reader should realize that the ground-work for successful
Slam bidding is laid in the *Opening bid* and the *early responses,* and that by the time a *game bid* has been reached
the partnership should have acquired a clear idea as to the
Slam possibilities of the hand.

In Part I it is assumed that neither side has scored
below the line. In Part II vulnerability is taken into consideration. The first chapters of Part III deal with the
bidding problems which arise when either or both sides
have partial scores. Another chapter is devoted to the
fascinating subject of Psychic bids. Part III also covers
psychological and partnership considerations.

Finally, the authors, recognizing the tremendous grow-
ing popularity of Duplicate Bridge and the fact that in
some respects Duplicate and Rubber Bridge are slightly

---

* For nearly two years the Four Aces have sponsored this principle,
while one leading system advocated light requirements for opening first
and second hand and heavier requirements for third and fourth hand, and
another leading system advocated just the reverse.

different games, have treated in Part III the special bidding situations encountered in Duplicate.

The bidding methods outlined in this book are in complete conformity with the new laws and scoring of Contract Bridge, which went into effect on March 31, 1935, and which will not be changed or revised until 1940.

We wish to acknowledge our debt of gratitude to Waldemar von Zedtwitz, one of the greatest Bridge analysts in the world, for his assistance as a collaborator and associate throughout the whole preparation of the book; to Richard L. Frey, a collaborator and former substitute on our team; to Harold S. Vanderbilt, the father of Contract Bridge, for his many valuable suggestions; to John R. Larus, Vice-President and Actuary of the Phoenix Mutual Life Insurance Company, for his thorough check of all the mathematical calculations, to Edward Hymes, Sr., Walter L. Pate and Stuyvesant Wainwright for their counsel, and to Richard H. Richardson, our secretary, not only for his tireless work but for his many practical suggestions incorporated in this book.

DAVID BURNSTINE
OSWALD JACOBY
MICHAEL T. GOTTLIEB
HOWARD SCHENKEN

The Four Aces Valuation Table

THIS Valuation Table is the fundamental basis of the Four Aces System and in a large measure is responsible for its success in competition against other systems, handicapped as they are by clumsy and inaccurate honor-trick tables, etc. Our Valuation Table is as follows:

Ace	3
King	2
Queen	1
Jack	½

Average Hand	6½—Total of Pack 26

Tables of High Card Requirements
OPENING BIDS
Classified by High Card Values

Holding:

0 to 3	Pass.
3½ to 6½	Pass or make a Pre-emptive bid.*
7 to 9	Pass or bid one of a suit.*
9½ or more	Some Opening bid is compulsory.
9½ to 11	Open with one of a suit.
11½ to 13	Open with one notrump if requirements are fulfilled; otherwise bid one or two of a suit.*
13½ or 14	Open with one or two of a suit.*

* Depending upon distribution, playing strength, etc., as discussed in the text of the book.

14½ to 16   Open with two notrump if requirements are
                        fulfilled; otherwise bid one or two of a suit.*
16½ to 18   Open with three notrump if requirements are
                        fulfilled; otherwise bid one or two of a suit.*
18½ or more Opening two-bid compulsory.

RESPONSES

High Card Requirements for Most Initial Responses
To an Opening Bid of One in a Suit **

Pass .... Less than 3½
One Notrump 3–6½
Single Raise in Partner's Suit 3–6½
One of a Suit (One-Over-One) .... 3 or more
Two of a Lower Ranking Suit .... 5 or more
Two Notrump 8½–10½
Three Notrump 10½–12
Jump to Three in Partner's Suit 6–10½

REBIDS

High Card Requirements for the Rebid in Notrump by a
Player Who has Opened with a Bid of One in a Suit **

One Notrump .... 11 or less
Two Notrump
  (a) Following a One-Over-One Response ⎤
  (b) Following a One-Notrump Response   ⎬ 12½–14
  (c) Following an Exploratory Response of
      Two in a Lower Ranking Suit 10½–12

Three Notrump
  (a) Following a One-Over-One Response ⎤
  (b) Following a One-Notrump Response   ⎬ 14½–16
  (c) Following an Exploratory Response of
      Two in a Lower Ranking Suit 12½–14

* Depending upon distribution, playing strength, etc., as discussed in
the text of the book.

** The exact requirements may be slightly varied in accordance with
common-sense dictates, as fully discussed in the text of the book.

Contents

CONTENTS   xxix

Part I

CHAPTER I

Theory of Opening Bids

ONE of the first problems confronting a player concerns the requirements for Opening bids. Turning to previous literature on the subject, he is soon lost in a maze of honor-trick tables, primary and secondary trick values, and so forth, which, when subjected to analysis, prove to be either inaccurate, incomplete, or too complicated for practical purposes; it also often causes the player to lose sight of the main object, which may be stated as follows:

OBJECT OF THE OPENING BID

The Opening bid should be made with a definite purpose and for a specific reason. High cards and distribution merely serve as a guide, both as to the measure of safety enjoyed, and the probable success of the undertaking. The bidding may be opened for one of several reasons:

(A) To launch the attack.

(B) To guard against being shut out by the adversaries.

(C) To obtain the most favorable lead against an anticipated adverse contract.

(D) To mislead the opponents or to interrupt their normal exchange of information.

Since bids under B, C, and D are of a specialized nature and are frequently made for tactical or positional reasons with hands below average, they will be treated in subsequent chapters, and the discussion here confined to the normal Opening bid * made for the purpose of initiating the exchange of information regarding an eventual part score, game or Slam contract. To justify an Opening bid in this connection, a hand must fulfill two main requirements, namely: high card strength and *adaptability to rebids*.

The first essential is that a hand contain a certain minimum of high cards, otherwise, it does not suggest immediate aggressive action. In deciding upon his proper procedure the player is advised, first, to compare his holding with the average hand, viz: an Ace, a King, a Queen, and a Jack, in order to form an initial general idea as to its strength and prospects. However, since the value of a hand, from which one of the four high honors is missing, cannot readily be compared with the average, we offer an extremely simple, yet concise and accurate valuation table to assist the player in gauging the strength of his hand.

This valuation table is the result of careful study and extensive calculations. It has been tested through a long period of successful rubber and tournament play, and found to be accurate. We use it as our basis and guide, and advise our readers to do likewise.

---

* As already stated, it is a principle of our system that the normal requirements for an Opening bid are the same whether in first, second, third or fourth position, and whether vulnerable or not vulnerable.

THE FOUR ACES VALUATION TABLE

Ace	3
King	2
Queen	I
Jack	½
	___
Total	6½

As the total high card value of the pack is 26, one fourth (the average hand) is 6½. This natural method of valuing a hand is the simplest ever devised. *It is impossible to play the Four Aces System with any other count or valuation.*

With this valuation table in mind, the next step is to classify the hand according to high card strength. Hands with 6½ or less, being average or below in high card strength, should ordinarily be passed. Hands with a high card value of from 7 to 9 are borderline and necessitate close analysis to determine the advisability of opening the bidding. Considerations of safety (distribution, length, and solidity of suit) and tactical reasons should be the determining factors. However, should the hand have a high card value of 9½ or more, it contains the equivalent of one whole Ace above average. Such holdings clearly demand attack and should be bid. They present but one problem—the choice of declaration.

Another consideration is that the hand should have a potential rebid. In its simplest form it may consist of the ability to rebid the initial declaration or conveniently and safely to show a second suit. In some cases the high card strength of the hand alone may warrant a rebid. Later when we consider specific examples of borderline and near-borderline hands, we shall show how the original bidder by means of the Principle of Anticipation should select an Opening bid which provides for a rebid.

> NOTE. *It is only necessary to guarantee a rebid over partner's temporary or game forcing response. A response by partner of one notrump or a single raise in your suit invites you to rebid only in case you hold substantial additional values to those shown by your Opening bid.*

This rebid feature is the foundation of the whole delicately balanced structure of our system and is the key to the smooth, easy and safe development of the bidding characteristic of the master player. Its meaning is easy to understand, and its absolute necessity will become apparent when we consider the problems of the Responding Hand. Opening the bidding without a sound rebid is as dangerous as lighting a short fuse to a charge of dynamite before locating the nearest exit.

THE OPENING BID WITH A STRONG HAND

It was previously pointed out that any hand with a high card value of 9½ (the value of an Ace above average) *must be bid,* irrespective of distribution or any other consideration.

With hands of such, or greater, high card strength, the Opening bid becomes strictly an offensive measure, even though it is possible, if partner has a "bust" or a very weak hand, that the opponents may be able to enter the bidding and eventually fulfill a contract. Accordingly, since the Opening bid with a hand of such power is an offensive bid, the most important consideration is to choose a bid which will make it most likely for the partnership to reach the proper final contract as easily and surely as possible.

There are five distinct Opening bids which may be used with a strong hand.

The first and strongest is the bid of two of a suit. While the holding for such a bid occurs very infrequently, when one does appear it is highly important that it should be handled correctly. With such a hand you have the power to compel your partner to give information about his hand even though it is a complete blank. The suit two-bid says: "Partner, my hand is so strong in high cards and in playing strength that I expect to make game, irrespective of your holding. However, as I desire an opportunity for the exchange of information at a low range, I am making this bid with the definite understanding that we must not stop at a contract of less than game, unless we should choose instead to double an overcall by a rash opponent."

The second is the three-notrump bid. This is similar to the suit two-bid in that it indicates a hand which will probably produce game without any assistance from partner. Here the resemblance ends, since an Opening three-notrump bid asks for no information from partner unless he cares to give it voluntarily. It follows that any response to the three-notrump bid must be regarded as a Slam invitation, and definitely not as a rescue.

The third bid is a younger brother of the three notrump—the two-notrump bid. Partner may pass an Opening two-notrump bid, but holding as much as a King, or a Queen and a Jack, or distributional advantages, he must respond.

The fourth is the one-notrump bid which, naturally, is the baby of the notrump family. Unlike his older brothers, whose appearances are rare, he is seen quite often and when he does put in an appearance, he must be recognized and partner should be apprised of his presence.

He is not particularly hard to recognize as he has four very distinctive features. The first is his distribution, which must be 4-3-3-3, 4-4-3-2 or 5-3-3-2. With any other distribution a hand is sufficiently unbalanced to indicate clearly that the bidding will develop properly only through an Opening suit bid.

The second feature is general preparation and protection. We should have some support for any suit partner might choose to bid, or protection against any opening lead by our opponent on the left.

The third feature is definite information to partner that he can afford to pass your bid without worrying about missing a game, if he holds no more than the equivalent of two Kings and no long biddable suit.

The fourth feature is playing strength. When you open with a bid of one notrump, you should be prepared for the possibility of having to play it doubled without suffering serious loss. Therefore, you should have a reasonable expectation of developing five tricks without any assistance from partner.

We come now to the fifth and most important bid of all —the *one-bid in a suit*. For every hand that should be bid originally as two of a suit or in notrump there are dozens that should be opened at one of a suit. Any hand strong enough for an Opening attacking bid which fails to meet all the requirements for a suit two-bid or a one-, two- or three-notrump bid should be bid as one of a suit.

The reader will note that Opening suit bids of three or more have been completely ignored in this chapter. The reason is that such bids, although of an attacking nature, are made on the theory that the best defense is a quick attack, and are made only when the strength of the hand is so concentrated in one suit that it offers few or no actual trick-taking possibilities against an opponent's contract.

BORDERLINE BIDS

Between the hands valued at 6½ or less, which should be passed, and those valued at 9½ or more, which should be bid, lies the very important borderline group. With a value of 7 to 9, inclusive, our first problem is not what to bid, but rather whether to bid or to pass.

A great many hands may be bid for tactical or positional reasons. Such bids will be discussed in Part II. The hands considered here are those which occur most frequently, such as:

♠ A K 10 x x   ♡ A J x   ◇ x x x   ♣ x x

High card value 8½.

This is a hand within the borderline zone, which is an obvious one-spade bid.

Let us discuss the considerations underlying our procedure with one of these normal hands. The first consideration is where, exactly, in the 7 to 9 zone does it fall? For instance, if its value is 9, we are within a Jack of having a compulsory opening bid and should be able to find one. On the other hand, if the value is but 7, it is only a Jack above average. Such hands should be passed in nearly all cases.

The second consideration is our holding of tens and nines. Such cards are not definitely valued, but, particularly when combined with higher honors, they strengthen a hand appreciably. For instance, A J 10 9 2 is considerably stronger than A J 8 7 2, and the additional strength may frequently be the determining factor in justifying a bid.

The third consideration is distribution. The presence of a six-card suit is of considerable offensive value, and a hand with a five-card suit is certainly preferable to one with but a four-carder. A void or a singleton always indicates a possible fit in one of the other suits and the concentration of nine or more cards in two suits greatly increases offensive power.

The fourth consideration is the strength of the suit to be bid. While the Opening bid is attacking, it must be borne in mind that the opponents may secure the contract, in which case your bid may indicate to partner a trick-saving lead.

The fifth consideration, although a phase of the first four, is the actual determining factor in deciding whether or not to open the bidding with a borderline hand. It is the rebid. Under our system, a player who opens the bidding with one of a suit promises to make a second bid if partner responds in another suit. *Hence, unless we can rebid over partner's response in any other suit all borderline hands should be passed.*

The above is part of the Principle of Anticipation, since the fact that we are prepared to rebid *anticipates* a response from partner. Suppose we hold:

♠ A K 7 2 (5)   ♡ 9 7 5 4   ◇ 9   ♣ A J 8 4 (3½)

Total value 8½.

With four cards of each major suit and a singleton diamond the hand shows definite possibilities. Accordingly, we decide to open the bidding. Most players would bid one spade without giving the situation much thought. However, a little deliberation will show that bid to be inadvisable. Should it be made, there is great likelihood

that partner will respond with two diamonds. If so—
what then? The hand is entirely too weak to consider
bidding two notrump or three clubs. A rebid of the four-
card spade suit would be equally as bad as a bid of
hearts on four to the nine-spot. A pass of the two-diamond
bid would break our pledge to partner to rebid over his
bid in another suit. Therefore, instead of opening the
bidding with one spade, we bid one club. Now it is impossible for partner to make an embarrassing response. If he
bids one diamond, we can well afford to reply with one
spade, thus rebidding at the level of one. If he bids a heart
or a spade, we simply raise his suit; while if he responds
with one notrump or two clubs, we pass. Incidentally,
when we come to Responses it will be shown that one notrump is a very unlikely response to an Opening one-club
bid.

The sixth test in opening borderline hands is the possibility of game. Unless our hand shows such a possibility,
in combination with some hypothetical holding by partner
with which he cannot afford to open the bidding, we should
pass.

Before presenting further examples we must inform
the reader that there is no certainty as to the best procedure to follow with a borderline hand, and to point out
that generally neither a pass nor a bid may be criticized
severely.

EXAMPLES OF BORDERLINE HANDS

Examples of hands with value of 9:

♠ A 6 5 (3)   ♡ A 7 2 (3)   ◇ A 8 2 (3)   ♣ 6 5 4 3

This hand should be passed. Here we have no favorable
distribution, no tens or nines, no length or strength in any

suit, and, most important of all, no trick-taking possibilities other than three blank Aces.

♠ A 3 2 (3)   ♡ A 3 2 (3)   ◇ A 7 6 5 2 (3)   ♣ 7 6

Although we have exactly the same high card holding as in the preceding example, the five-card diamond suit, headed by the Ace, indicates a substantially greater playing strength, and hence is the determining factor in making this hand a proper Opening one-diamond bid.

♠ A K 10 9 6 5 (5)   ♡ A Q 6 (4)   ◇ 3 2   ♣ 3 2

A hand such as this, even though its high card holding falls in the "7 to 9" zone, is not at all borderline, but is a very strong Opening bid.

Examples of hands with value of 8½:

♠ A J 8 7 2 (3½)   ♡ A K 2 (5)   ◇ 8 5 4   ♣ 7 3

We have a fairly good five-card spade suit which we are prepared to rebid. An Opening bid is indicated.

♠ K 9 6 2 (2)   ♡ K 9 6 5 (2)   ◇ K 10 9 (2)   ♣ K J (2½)

This hand is well stocked with tens and nines but has no five-card suit, no singleton, and no biddable suit, and certainly no rebid. Furthermore, the hand has an additional weakness which lies in the fact that its shortest suit is the strongest in high cards. This additional weakness is slight, but nevertheless is the deciding factor in passing this hand.

♠ K 6 2 (2)   ♡ K 9 6 5 (2)   ◇ K 9 (2)   ♣ K J 10 9 (2½)

This hand is the same as the preceding one except that the ten of diamonds and the nine of spades have become clubs. We now have a sound one-club bid. If our partner responds with one diamond, we bid one notrump, while if he responds with one heart we have a very sound two-heart bid. Over a spade response, we have a choice between one notrump and two spades, either bid being quite satisfactory, while if partner bids two clubs or one notrump we pass.

Examples of hands with value of 8:

With but a value of 8, we should be very careful of four-card suit bids. With a sound five-card suit, we will be able to open, since we can rebid the suit. Examples of such hands are:

♠ A Q 6 5 4 (4)   ♡ A Q 2 (4)   ◊ 10 6 2   ♣ 8 6

Bid one spade.

♠ 6 2   ♡ A K 10 4 3 (5)   ◊ A 2 (3)   ♣ 5 4 3 2

Bid one heart.

With a value of $7\frac{1}{2}$, the four-card suit bid is almost entirely eliminated. With only a Queen above average, you must have a strong suit or you should not open the bidding.

♠ A Q 9 8 2 (4)   ♡ A J 2 ($3\frac{1}{2}$)   ◊ 10 6 2   ♣ 8 6

Bid one spade. The strength of our suit justifies the opening.

Examples of hands with value of 7:

These hands are so slightly above average that to justify a bid we must have either a strong five-card suit or a good six-card suit. Even then to bid is always questionable.

♠ A K Q 7 5 4 (6)   ♡ Q 6 2 (1)   ◊ 7 5   ♣ 8 4

The exceptionally strong spade suit justifies an Opening bid.

♠ 9 7   ♡ K Q 10 9 6 (3)   ◊ A Q 10 5 (4)   ♣ 6 5

The concentration of strength plus the tens and nines makes this hand a one-heart bid.

The reader will note from the examples of Opening bids given in this chapter that under our system we do not pass strong hands. Hence, there is no need for Third or Fourth Hand to make a light Opening bid to protect a possible big hand that we have passed, and at the same time there is no necessity for First or Second Hand to make a light opening, fearing that partner will pass out a game in third or fourth position.

CHAPTER II

Opening Bid of One of a Suit with a Strong Hand

As ALREADY emphasized, the main requirement for an Opening bid is the ability to rebid. In our discussion of borderline hands we pointed out that without the rebid feature the hand should be passed. With the hands to be discussed in this chapter, we start with the premise that an Opening bid must be made. Hence we select a bid which will permit us to make a rebid, keeping in mind that we merely promise to rebid over a response in a new suit or Jump bid by partner and that a response of either one notrump or of two in our suit may be passed by us.

Since Contract Bridge supplanted Auction Bridge it has been necessary to give more consideration to the essential differences between the various suits. The first difference is between the major suits (spades and hearts) and the minor suits (diamonds and clubs). It requires ten tricks to make game in a major suit, while eleven are needed for game in a minor, and but nine at notrump. Consequently, were it not for the advantage afforded by a favorable trump declaration, game contracts would generally be played at notrump. It has been demonstrated that this trump advantage is worth, on the average, slightly more than one trick. Therefore, when a fit is found

15

in a major suit, the hand, if played at game, should generally be played in that suit. In the minor suits this only applies if there is reason to believe that the trump advantage will be worth a full two tricks, or if the bidding discloses a suit unstopped or stopped but once, thereby making notrump play unsafe. In the event that your long minor suit is solid, one stopper in each of the other suits is generally sufficient to make a game contract in notrump safe.

It is generally impossible to tell in advance of the play of a particular hand exactly how many extra tricks a favorable trump will produce, but in most instances there will be certain definite indications. For instance, should our partner bid a suit, our holding of four cards in that suit indicates a fit and an advantage, if played in that suit, of from one to two tricks over notrump. Accordingly, when a major suit is bid originally, it should have sufficient strength so that the bidder will be prepared to play the hand for game in that suit with but four small in partner's hand. If the bidder holds any five trumps, he is reasonably well protected since even if the opponents hold the Ace, King, Queen and Jack there is a chance that all four will fall in two leads and that consequently but two trump tricks will be lost. If the original bidder has but four trumps, in order to have a reasonably good expectation of not losing more than two trump tricks, a fairly substantial high card holding is necessary. Experience has shown the minimum holding to be A-10, K-10, or Q-J.

MINIMUM BIDDABLE MAJOR SUITS

The reference to the loss of two trump tricks when game is contracted for in a major does not mean that game should always be bid in a major in preference to notrump when there is a likelihood of losing two trump tricks. What it does mean is that if the original bidder has the minimum possible trump strength for an Opening bid in a major and partner has the minimum possible trump support to warrant a game contract in the suit, it should appear to be highly improbable that more than two trump tricks will be lost. Of course, if each player has the minimum possible trump strength, the combined hands must have such great strength in the side suits that there is little likelihood of losing more than one trick in the other three suits.

As it is improbable that both the original bidder and his partner will have minimum trump holdings, the situation in which the loss of two trump tricks must be considered will occur infrequently.

Rule One. The minimum for a biddable major suit by Opening hand is:

1. Any holding of five or more cards.
2. Any holding of four cards as good as:
   - (a) A 10 3 2
   - (b) K 10 3 2
   - (c) Q J 3 2

MINIMUM BIDDABLE MINOR SUITS

If we open the bidding with a minor suit it will rarely happen that our partner will insist that we contract for game in that suit. He may strongly invite us to do so, but should we shift to notrump he will insist on the minor only if he has a very strong holding in that suit (certainly as many as five) in addition to other distributional values if played in the minor.

With this in mind we can greatly reduce our suit requirements for an original minor suit bid.

Rule Two. A three-card suit in either minor headed by the Ace or King, or one of four cards in either minor irrespective of tops, is biddable.

For years a willingness to bid such three-card or nearly worthless four-card minor suits has constituted an important part of the expert's margin of superiority over other players. Now for the first time the theory is incorporated in a bidding system.

Of course, bids of this type should not be made in preference to other and more orthodox bids. However, there are two instances when their use is absolutely essential, namely:

(a) We have no properly biddable suit, but are too strong in high cards to pass and too weak to bid one notrump.

(b) We have no properly biddable suit and are too strong in high cards to bid one notrump * and too weak to bid two notrump.

Examples are as follows:

♠ A x x **   ♡ J x x x   ◊ A x x   ♣ A x x

High card value 9½.

Bid one club, intending to bid one notrump over a bid of one diamond or one spade by partner, and two hearts should he bid one heart.

---

* Under our system the Opening one-notrump is conservative and its meaning is strictly limited. The bid indicates a hand with high card values substantially greater than those necessary for a hand which justifies an Opening bid of one of a suit. Also there is a gap between the maximum one-notrump and the minimum two-notrump bids.

** Any card below ten is indicated by x.

♠ A K x   ♡ A x x x   ◇ A x x   ♣ x x x

High card value 11.

Bid one diamond, intending to bid two spades or two hearts over a response in either of those suits by partner, and being quite willing to bid two notrump if partner's response is two clubs.

♠ A K x   ♡ A x x x   ◇ A J x   ♣ A x x

High card value 14½, with 6 honors.

This hand, which is too weak for a two-notrump bid and too strong for a one-notrump, should be bid one club.

ONE-SUIT HANDS

One-suit hands such as the following

♠ A x   ♡ K Q J x x   ◇ A x x   ♣ x x x

High card value 9½

♠ A K x x x   ♡ A x x   ◇ K x x   ♣ x x

High card value 10.

offer no particular problem in selecting a bid.

TWO-SUIT HANDS

If we hold as many as 11 cards in two suits our hand is a "freak two-suiter." A discussion of bidding methods with such hands is included in Part II. This chapter deals only with two four-card suits, a four- and a five-card suit, a four- and a six-card suit, and two five-card suits.

In the case of the six and four we must always bid the six-card suit first and in general plan to bid it a second time before showing our four-carder. As a matter of fact, with such hands we may never bid our four-card suit at all.

With a two-suiter of five each, the higher ranking suit should be bid first.

When holding a five- and a four-card suit the general rule is: Bid the five-card suit first. However, there is a very important exception, namely: In case the five-card suit ranks immediately below the four-card suit, and the shorter suit is strong in high cards, it frequently will be found advisable to bid the four-card suit first because there will probably be no opportunity to show it later

There remains the hand with two four-card suits. Here the problem of which suit to bid first is determined entirely by the Principle of Anticipation. We should assume that our partner will respond with a bid of our weakest suit and we should choose for our Opening bid the suit which will enable us to know what to do if our partner responds unfavorably. If our two suits rank in succession we should bid the higher one first, since our partner's response in another suit will always permit us to bid the lower one. If our two suits are spades and clubs we should bid the clubs first unless our hand is strong enough to warrant our bidding two notrump or three clubs on the second round.

Where the choice lies between spades and diamonds, or hearts and clubs, it becomes somewhat more difficult, and preparation for either of the other two suits may be the guiding factor. For example, holding

$$\spadesuit \ Jxx \qquad \heartsuit \ AKxx \qquad \diamondsuit \ xx \qquad \clubsuit \ AQxx$$

our proper Opening bid is one club, since, should we bid the heart originally, we would have no appropriate rebid over a two-diamond response. But, holding

$$\spadesuit \ AQxx \qquad \heartsuit \ Jxx \qquad \diamondsuit \ AKxx \qquad \clubsuit \ xx$$

we would bid one spade, now being prepared to bid two diamonds over partner's two-club response, or three hearts over his two-heart response. Whereas if we bid one diamond, the response of two clubs would place us in an awkward position, since we would not care to rebid our four-card diamond suit, and two-notrump is not warranted by our holding; while a two-spade bid would shut out a return to diamonds at the level of two.

It will pay the reader to master the preceding principles because they will pilot him across a sea which has never been charted and is known only to expert players. It is so rough and stormy that even they cannot navigate it without some risk of running their ships into the Scylla of the underbid or the Charybdis of the misfit.

A complete discussion as to the choice of a particular suit in preference to another will be of greater value after we have covered the Theory of Responses.

EXAMPLES OF TWO-SUIT HANDS

The following examples of hands with two properly biddable suits are given without other comment than to point out which should be bid first. After we have discussed the Theory of Responses and have come to the development of the bidding, we shall repeat all these examples, showing how the bidding develops if the proper suit has first been chosen.

♠ A K x x (5)   ♡ Q J 10 x x x (1½)   ◊ A x (3)   ♣ x
Total value of hand is 9½. Bid one heart.

♠ K J x x x (2½)   ♡ A x (3)   ◊ A K x x x (5)   ♣ x
Total value of the hand is 10½. Bid one spade.

♠ K Q J x (3½)   ♡ A K x x x (5)   ◊ Q x (1)   ♣ x x
Total value of the hand is 9½. Bid one spade.

♠ K Q J x (3½) ♡ K Q J x x (3½) ◇ A x (3) ♣ K x (2)
Total value of the hand is 12. Bid one heart.

♠ x x   ♡ A K x x (5)   ◇ A Q x x (4)   ♣ J x x (½)
Total value of the hand is 9½. Bid one heart.

♠ A K x x (5)   ♡ x x   ◇ x x x   ♣ A K x x (5)
Total value of the hand is 10. Bid one club.

♠ A K x x (5)   ♡ x   ◇ A Q J x (4½)   ♣ x x x x
Total value of the hand is 9½. Bid one diamond.

♠ A K x x (5)   ♡ x x x   ◇ K Q x x (3)   ♣ K 10 (2)
Total value of the hand is 10. Bid one spade.

In connection with two-suit hands there is an interesting modification of the order in which biddable suits should be called, which is as follows:

If our hand contains two four-card suits successive in rank such as spades and hearts, hearts and diamonds, or diamonds and clubs, it is permissible, for the purpose of providing a rebid, to shade the biddable suit requirements of the higher ranking suit, reserving the lower ranking suit as our rebid. Examples are as follows:

♠ A 9 7 3   ♡ A K Q 2   ◇ J x x   ♣ x x

High card value 9½.

Bid one spade, since we are now prepared to bid two hearts in reply to a two-diamond or two-club response by partner.

♠ x x x   ♡ Q 10 x x   ◇ A K x x   ♣ A J

High card value 9½.

Bid one heart. If the Opening were one diamond there would be no satisfactory second bid over a two-club response by partner.

THREE-SUIT HANDS

Hands with three strong suits occur very rarely. They are so powerful distributionally that it is frequently necessary for the player with such a holding to shade his biddable suit requirements. With 4-4-4-1, assuming that all three suits are either properly biddable or almost so, we select for our first bid that suit which ranks immediately below that of the singleton. The following examples will be discussed again under Development of the Bidding.

> NOTE: *If one of the three suits is distinctly not biddable (J x x x) the hand should be bid as a two-suiter.*

♠ AK32   ♡ A932   ◇ 6   ♣ QJ32
Bid one club.

♠ AK32   ♡ x   ◇ KJxx   ♣ AKxx
Bid one diamond.

♠ A10xx   ♡ AQxx   ◇ AQxx   ♣ x
Bid one spade.*

With 5-4-4-0, bid the five-card suit first. Example:

♠ —   ♡ AQxx   ◇ QJ10xx   ♣ AKxx
Bid one diamond.

* For the purpose of this bid, spades are considered to rank immediately below clubs.

CHAPTER III

The Opening Bid of One Notrump *

IN THE preceding chapters we have discussed the Opening bid of one of a suit. It has been pointed out that a suit bid of one should be made with a hand only slightly above the average in high card strength, if strong in distributional values. We have noted that as the distribution of the hand becomes more balanced, additional high card strength is necessary to warrant opening the bidding.

The strength ranges from hands only slightly above average to hands so strong as probably to produce game with practically no assistance from partner. Because of this wide variation in strength, partner is expected to respond to a suit bid of one with no more than a King and a Queen or their equivalent.

The Opening one-notrump bid cannot be used to cover such a wide range, and by its very nature belongs in the class of Limiting bids. Our experience has demonstrated that the proper limits in high card strength are 11½

* For no apparent reason, the one-notrump bid has become the football of the "system manufacturers." One writer recommends a notrump so gigantic that a pass by partner is practically criminal; while another recommends one so pitifully weak that partner cannot afford to raise without holding the equivalent of an Opening bid. Instead of approaching the subject logically, they seem merely to have striven to differ with one another. Our theory of the Opening one-notrump has been successful under many severe tests, since it is based entirely on logical considerations.

minimum and 13 maximum. These limits have not been
selected arbitrarily. They have been fixed only after much
study of the problems involved. *In addition to qualifying
in high card strength the bid should be reserved for those
hands which if bid originally as one of a suit would probably create a future problem that would not loom up to
embarrass us if the Opening bid were one notrump.*

The reader should bear in mind that the 11½ to 13
limits are not absolutely inflexible. In actual play we deem
it wise, at times, to deviate slightly either from the upper
or lower limit. In general, however, it will be found good
policy to conform to the standard.

In Chapter I it was pointed out that the Opening one-
notrump bid should be made only with a hand that contains one of three distributions, namely: 4-3-3-3, 4-4-3-2
or 5-3-3-2. Therefore, when a player opens with one notrump, he should anticipate the likelihood that the final
contract will be a notrump declaration.

In the Four Aces Valuation Table no value is assigned
to the tens. *In notrump hands, the tens take on a distinct
value.* At a suit contract the third lead of any suit will
probably be trumped and the trick lost. At notrump, ability
to win the third lead of a suit is very important, as is also
the winning of the fourth. In this connection the ten-spot
becomes of definite worth, while the relative importance
of the Jack and/or the Queen, as contrasted with the
Ace, is considerably increased.

This difference in values is determined in the following manner: A notrump hand in addition to being above
average in high card strength should also be above the
average in the *number of honors held,* and for this purpose the ten becomes an honor, although not counted in
determining high card values. The average honor holding

is one Ace, one King, one Queen, one Jack and one ten, a total of five. The Opening notrump should generally include at least seven honors. In case a hand has less than seven honors, ½ *point should be subtracted* from the high card value of the hand for each honor less than seven held, while conversely, ½ point should be added for each honor in excess of seven. The nines and eights also have more definite importance in the notrump picture, and while they are assigned no mathematical value, the player should make a habit of considering their presence or absence in any hand that is of doubtful notrump qualifications.

At about this point many readers will ask: "Why use the one-notrump bid at all? It is certainly possible to find a suit bid in practically every hand that answers the requirements for an Opening one-notrump bid."

The answer to this question lies first in the *Principle of Anticipation*. Consider the following hand:

♠ K 7 (2)   ♡ A 9 7 3 (3)   ◇ A K 10 3 (5)   ♣ K 10 9 (2)

A total value of 12. As the hand includes exactly seven honors there is no adjustment. This hand also meets all the requirements for an Original one-diamond bid.

Let us consider what happens if one diamond is bid, and our partner responds with a bid of one notrump. Now we are in a quandary as to whether to rebid or to pass. If his response is on a bare King and Queen, the hand should be played at one notrump. If his response is on an Ace, a King and a Jack it is probable that three notrump can be made and consequently the hand should be played at that declaration.

If he responds to our bid of one diamond with one spade, we are likewise in a quandary. Our hand is too strong for a mere one-notrump bid and too weak to bid two no-trump. In fact, any bid except one-and-a-half notrump is decidedly unsatisfactory, and it so happens that a one-and-a-half notrump bid is not permitted under the rules.

On the other hand, if we open with one no-trump we have no future embarrassing problem to face. We know that if the final declaration is three notrump *a total valuation of 17½* in the combined hands will usually produce the necessary nine tricks. We have clearly shown our partner that we hold a count of from 11½ to 13. If he now makes any bid whatsoever we are prepared to continue.

Another answer to this question lies in the Principle of Preparation for the Lead. If the distribution of our hand is 4-3-3-3, 4-4-3-2 or 5-3-3-2, we must consider, irrespective of our Opening bid, that it is extremely probable that the final declaration will be notrump. In case our doubleton is King-small and our partner is the declarer, an opening lead through that holding might result in the opponents taking the first five or six tricks, while were we the declarer this could not happen.

This second Principle of Preparation for the Lead is of relatively small importance and should be given only minor consideration. Some players feel that any hand containing a tenace must be led up to and consequently feel justified in bidding notrump just because their hand contains Ace-Queen-small or King-Jack-small of some suit. Many players suffer from a notrump complex. This complex is one of the most dangerous bidding habits to acquire and we wish to warn against it. Remember, if a hand fulfills *all the requirements* for an Opening one-notrump bid it should be bid one notrump, otherwise not.

EXAMPLES OF ORIGINAL ONE-NOTRUMP BIDS

The following hands are examples of original one-no-trump bids.

♠ J 9 8 4 (½)   ♡ K Q J (3½)   ◊ A Q 7 (4)   ♣ K Q J (3½)

The total high card value of the hand is 11 ½, but since it includes nine honors, one point is added to give a no-trump value of 12 ½.

♠ A 8 4 (3)   ♡ A 8 4 2 (3)   ◊ A K 6 (5)   ♣ A 4 3 (3)

The total of this hand is 14, but as it includes only five honors, one point is deducted, leaving a net notrump value of 13. In this particular hand, the addition of one ten would give a notrump value of 13 ½, but even so one notrump should still be bid. The addition of a second ten would make the value 14 and in that case we should make some other bid, as the hand would then be too strong to risk the danger of our partner passing a bid of one notrump. The proper bid would be one of a suit, *not two notrump*. If a hand is just too strong to bid one notrump it does not necessarily justify a two-notrump bid. Instead we fall back on the reliable and ubiquitous suit bid even to the extent of bidding a three-card minor. (See Chapter II.) The reason for the selection of a suit bid is of course in full accord with the Principle of Anticipation, since if partner responds with one notrump, we are now prepared to raise him to two.

♠ J 10 3 2 (½)   ♡ Q 10 6 4 (1)   ◊ A Q (4)   ♣ A K 8 (5)

The total of this hand is 10 ½, but we have eight honors, making a notrump value of 11. Secondly, the Ace-Queen alone of diamonds is one of the combinations that we particularly desire to have led up to, so with this hand we shade our notrump requirements and bid one notrump in preference to one of a suit.

♠ A J (3½)   ♡ Q 9 3 (1)   ◇ A K 4 3 2 (5)   ♣ K J 7 (2½)

Total value 12, with seven honors. There is no adjustment. Bid one notrump.

Instead of giving more examples, we shall repeat the *requirements for a one-notrump bid.* The reader will find it profitable to set up his own examples. First the hand should have a *value of from 11½ to 13, and should include seven honors. For each honor held less than seven, ½ point should be subtracted and for each honor more than seven, ½ point added.*

Secondly, the distribution of the hand should be 4-3-3-3, 4-4-3-2 or 5-3-3-2.

Thirdly, a doubleton, if any, must include either the Ace or the King, and if there are two or more three-card suits in the hand, not more than one may be headed by a lower card than the Queen.

And finally, when a bid of one notrump is reserved for such hands, we give our partner the very definite and precise information that although we have a good sound hand, it is not a rock-crusher. There is no need for him to rescue us, and unless his hand contains definite values, he may pass without fear of missing a game. Hence, we gain the further advantage of knowing that if he responds to our one-notrump, his strength is definitely more than the minimum required for a response to one of a suit.

CHAPTER IV

Opening Forcing and Strength-Showing Bids *

OPENING bids of more than one are a nuisance in bidding because they interrupt the natural easy exchange of information between partners. For that reason they should be employed only to safeguard against the possibility of misfortune. As the total high card value of the entire pack is constant ** it necessarily follows that the greater the strength of any one hand the weaker must be the other three. As a corollary, the stronger our hand the greater is the chance that our partner will pass an Opening one bid—hence the necessity for the employment of some method, even at the cost of crowding the bidding, to insure against a pass by partner. The best means yet devised is the use of the Opening *Forcing* and *Strength-Showing* bids.

With a hand so strong that we fear a certain, or almost certain, game or Slam may be lost as the result of the passing out of a one-bid, it is essential that we open with

---

* There will be a further discussion of these bids following the chapter on Slam bidding.

** Some authorities, by a mysterious hocus-pocus of their own, vary the high card or honor-trick value of the pack by as much as 40 percent from deal to deal. With us, two and two always make four, and in each deal there are always four Aces, four Kings, four Queens and four Jacks, or a total value of 26.

30

a strong bid, one which partner will recognize as Forcing or nearly so. There are three such bids at our disposal:

1. The Suit Two-Bid.
2. The Three-Notrump Bid.
3. The Two-Notrump Bid.

These three bids each impart a very similar message and the correct choice is frequently difficult to make. However, if the reader will bear in mind the following principles, he should be able to make the correct decision in most instances:

The Two-Bid. This bid may be made with any hand which we desire to play at game, irrespective of what our partner holds. It must fulfill *both* of the following requirements.

(a) A probable playing strength of within one trick of game.

(b) A substantial high card strength—generally at least 13, but which may occasionally be reduced to 11 with freak hands such as:

♠ x   ♡ A K x x x x x   ◇ A x   ♣ A x

High card value 11.

♠ —   ♡ A K Q x x x   ◇ x   ♣ A K x x x x

High card value 11.

An opening two-bid imposes a definite obligation on us and our partner to continue the bidding until game is reached, except in the event that an adverse overcall offers an opportunity to double for a worthwhile penalty. Even if we have a Grand Slam in our own hand, we may start with a two-bid, hoping eventually to be doubled at seven.

The Three-Notrump Bid. This bid is made with a hand that we desire to play at game irrespective of what partner may hold. Like all notrump bids, it gives special information, in that it tells partner that although we can probably make game irrespective of what he holds, that we have no long suit, and can make a Slam only if he holds either a long suit or two or three high cards.

The Two-Notrump Bid. This bid shows a hand that is almost strong enough to bid three notrump. However, the Opening two-notrump bid does not guarantee game and should be passed by a partner with a blank hand. The minimum high card strength that partner needs to raise an Opening bid of two notrump is one King, or a Queen and a Jack.

The correct choice of these three bids will come with experience. However, we shall give a few simple rules, followed by a number of examples.

1. Bid two notrump with a stopper in every suit, a high card value of from 14½ to 16, and one of the following distributions: 4-3-3-3, 4-4-3-2 or 5-3-3-2.

2. Bid three notrump with a similar hand, but with a high card value of from 16½ to 18. Seven honors is normal for any Opening bid in the notrump family.

3. Bid two of a suit with any other exceptionally strong hand fulfilling both playing strength and high card requirements.

EXAMPLES OF FORCING BIDS

Examples of Forcing and almost Forcing bids:

♠ A Q   ♡ A K x x   ◇ A K x x   ♣ A 10 x

High card value 17 with 8 honors.

Bid three notrump. Nothing is to be gained by bidding

two diamonds or two hearts with this hand, because unless partner holds either some high cards or a long suit we
are unlikely to make a Slam. Furthermore, if we should
open with a suit two-bid * and partner should respond with
two notrump, showing a bust, we should have to bid three
notrump. In this instance, a spade lead through the Ace-
Queen might wreck the hand, while if we are the notrump
bidder this danger is eliminated and the game is almost
certain.

♠ A J x   ♡ K x   ◊ A K Q x x   ♣ A x x

High card value 14½ with 7 honors.

This is a sound Opening two-notrump bid.

♠ A K Q J x   ♡ A K Q J x   ◊ x x x   ♣ —

High card value 13.

Bid two spades. We do not wish to play this hand short
of game, and if partner can take care of two of our diamond losers we are sure of a Slam.

♠ A K Q   ♡ A Q 10   ◊ A K x   ♣ A K x x

High card value 20 with 10 honors.

Bid two clubs. There are a great many hands with which
partner would pass an Opening three-notrump bid, but
which, combined with this tremendous hand, would produce a Slam.

♠ K Q J x x x   ♡ A Q J x x x   ◊ x   ♣ —

High card value 8.

Bid one spade. Although this hand shows distinct Slam
possibilities, certain key cards are required in partner's

---

* With a notrump pattern, we reserve the use of the two-bid for hands
where the high card value is greater than 18 (the upper limit of the
Opening three-notrump bid).

hand. Furthermore, there is no reason to expect that a
one-bid will be passed all around the table; and thirdly,
after an Opening one-bid, if we eventually reach a high
contract, there is greater likelihood of a Double by an over-
eager opponent.

♠ —   ♡ A K x x   ◇ A K x x   ♣ A K Q x x

High card value 16.

Bid two clubs.

♠ x   ♡ A K x x   ◇ A K x x   ♣ A K x x

High card value 15.

Bid one heart. The hand is definitely not strong enough to
make an Opening Forcing bid.

♠ A K Q J x x x   ♡ A x x   ◇ A x   ♣ x

High card value 12½.

Bid two spades. With 9 certain tricks we definitely want to
reach a game bid. Furthermore, the holding by partner
of King-Queen-Jack-small in either hearts or diamonds
will produce a Slam.

♠ A K J   ♡ A K x x x   ◇ A   ♣ K Q 10 x

High card value 16½.

Bid two hearts. This hand fully satisfies the requirements
for an Opening two-bid, although not a strong one. The
singleton Ace of diamonds makes an Opening two- or three-
notrump bid inadvisable.

♠ K J x   ♡ K Q x   ◇ A J x   ♣ A K x x

High card value 14 with 8 honors (e.g. 14½)

Bid two notrump. This hand barely fulfills the requirements for an Opening two-notrump bid.

CHAPTER V

The First Response to an Opening Suit Bid

THEORY OF THE FIRST RESPONSE

IN THE preceding chapters we have considered the problem of the Opening bid from two angles:

1. Whether to bid or to pass.
2. Having decided to bid, what to bid.

We have shown that we are guided in our action, first, by the actual high card strength and, secondly, by rebid potentialities, as the determining factors. The first response must be viewed from the same angles:

1. To respond or to pass.
2. Having decided to respond, what to bid.

In responding we need hardly consider the first, as experience has shown that while most hands do not warrant an Opening bid, practically every hand warrants a response. Furthermore, while the Opening bid should always be viewed by partner as an aggressive move, certain responses, while constructive in character, may invite an early discontinuance of the attack.

It is difficult to generalize much further on the Theory of the Response, since obviously the response to one no-trump presents a problem different from the response to a suit bid, and even different suit bids present different

35

responding problems. However, we wish to point out that our general principles in this respect are as follows:

I. *Limits.* There are two main classes of responses:

1. The Limiting Response which takes the form of confirmation of partner's bid by raising or by a bid of some number of notrumps, and which immediately places the strength of the Responding Hand within a certain very definite range, thereby giving the original bidder primary control of future developments.

2. The Exploratory Response which does not tend clearly to define the limits of the strength of the Responding Hand, but instead asks the Opening bidder for more information. This course of action is taken for the purpose of permitting the Responding Hand to assume control or to return it later to the original bidder, as may be indicated by the development of the bidding.

II. *Anticipation.* Since our first response will, in most instances, initiate a series of bids by us it is particularly important to choose that response which will as far as possible simplify our future problems, while at the same time giving information to our partner.

III. *Development and Forcing.* The Development Principle invites us to select that response which will allow us to sound out possibilities at a low range in the bidding. Our Forcing Principle makes this slow development possible.

IV. *Safety.* Any response should be safe from the possibility of a severe penalty at the level to which it forces, or at the contract it tentatively suggests as final.

RESPONSES TO AN OPENING BID OF ONE OF A SUIT

The action to be taken by the Responding player will fall under one of five headings:

1. The Pass.
2. Temporary Forces (One-Over-One bids and Takeouts in two of a lower ranking suit—the Exploratory Responses).
3. Raises.
4. Notrump Takeouts.
5. Slam Invitational Game Forces.

Considered in order of strength these responses may be classified as follows:

1. Limiting bids made with weak holdings to provide partner with an opportunity to rebid (the Chance).
2. Neutral bids which compel a temporary continuation of the bidding without immediately indicating how weak or how strong the Responding Hand may be (the One-Over-One).
3. Strong neutral bids which also force a temporary continuation of the bidding, but at the same time indicate that the Responding Hand holds as a minimum certain well defined values (the bid of two of a lower ranking suit).
4. Forces committing the partnership to a game or Slam contract (Jump bids in any suit or notrump).

The possibilities of all partnership holdings which do not immediately reveal themselves as perfect fits should be delicately explored at the lowest possible range in order to avoid arriving at premature decisions.

The One-Over-One Response assumes a multiple nature. It may be a weak response, largely negative in character and given merely in the nature of a Chance. With slightly stronger holdings it explores the possibilities of game at a low range in the bidding, while with very strong hands it constitutes the first step in unfolding the picture. Takeouts made at the level of two show a certain amount of strength which subsequent bids will limit. All notrump bids show a definite minimum and maximum holding. Raises show a combination of high cards and distributional advantages. Slam Invitational Game Forces have no upper limit of strength.

Our reasoning in selecting the first response is similar to that employed in selecting our Opening bid. We must first consider the high card strength and the distributional picture of our own hand in order to determine whether or not to take action, and if so, whether weak or strong. Having decided affirmatively, we will nearly always have a choice between a Limiting Response (a raise in suit or a bid of any number of notrump) and an Exploratory response (a bid in another suit).

It is very important that the correct choice be made. The lesson can best be learned by studying specific cases, bearing in mind that:

A Limiting Response is made:

    (a) To give our partner an accurate picture of our high card strength and distribution. This is accomplished by bidding one or more notrump; or

    (b) To give a tentative picture of our trick-taking strength in support of partner's bid, with the intention of directing him to take control of subsequent bidding. This is done by means of one or more raises in partner's suit; while

An Exploratory Response is made when we definitely wish either to reserve primary control or are uncertain whether it should be in our hand or partner's.

The normal responses to an Opening suit bid of one are as follows:

1. The pass.

2. *The bid of one of a higher ranking suit.* This is the well-known One-Over-One, probably the most misunderstood of all bids in Contract Bridge. Certain systemists have made of it a fetish, and numberless persons claim to have invented it and to have been the first to use it. As a matter of fact, it was invented in a manner similar to that of cooked meat. Cooked meat is superior to raw meat, yet nobody knows who first subjected it to heat, unless we accept as true the humorous version given by Charles Lamb in his "Dissertation upon Roast Pig."

The One-Over-One is Forcing to the extent that after such a response the bidding must be continued at least as high as one notrump. The One-Over-One is the most delicate instrument in the expert's tool chest. With a very strong hand he may respond with a One-Over-One bid, and may trap an opponent who rashly overcalls. With a weak hand he may also make a One-Over-One bid without immediately disclosing his weakness. Thus, if the adversaries' strength is divided, neither may hold enough to enter the bidding safely. At the same time it allows him to secure additional information concerning partner's hand at a low range in the bidding. It is very important that the reader should master our version of this phase of the bidding. As previously stated a One-Over-One response does not force the bidding beyond one notrump. Hence, to make such a response very little strength is necessary. As a matter of fact, with a weak hand the One-Over-One bid is preferable to a one-notrump response as it conceals your weakness from the player on the left; and at the same time it allows you to drop the bidding at one notrump or two of a suit.

3. *The One Notrump Response.* This response definitely indicates a weak hand and is made merely for the purpose of permitting the original bidder to continue in whatever manner he deems best. It is made with a high card value of from 3 to 6½ and says in effect: "Partner, I have considered your Opening bid and, while I do not think we can make a game, unless your hand is very strong, nevertheless, even if you have only a minimum bid I feel we will be reasonably safe at a one-notrump contract."

4. *The Immediate Single Raise in the Suit Bid.* Like the one notrump, this is a weak response, but is slightly more encouraging. Although in general it shows the same high card limits (3 to 6½) there are cases where such a raise is proper, with fine distribution and no high card strength at all, while there are rare cases where no other sound bid can be found with a high card value of as much as 8.

5. *Response of Two of a Lower Ranking Suit.* As our partner's Opening bid has indicated that he will rebid if we show a new suit, this bid, like the One-Over-One, is a Temporary Force. However, since it immediately takes the bidding into the range of two it should not be made with a weak hand.

6. *The Two-Notrump Response.* This is a Forcing bid to game, but at the same time it is strictly a limiting bid and shows a balanced hand with a high card value of

from 8½ to 10½. It does not absolutely guarantee game, but it does guarantee a good play for game.

7. *The Three-Notrump Response.* This bid is made with a balanced hand and a high card value of from 10½ to 12 and definitely guarantees game. At the same time it strongly invites partner to consider Slam possibilities.

In connection with the two- and three-notrump responses, the following three points should be borne in mind.

> (a) We may slightly vary our high card value either way, depending upon the holding of tens and nines, and other qualities of the hand.
>
> (b) They indicate preparation for any lead and some slight support (at least J x or x x x) for partner's suit.
>
> (c) They should be made only after we have carefully considered and decided not to make an Exploratory Response.

8. *The Jump to Three of Partner's Opening Bid in a Major Suit.* This bid is forcing to game. While not inviting a Slam, it shows both good trump support and a substantial high card holding (6 or better in most instances). It allows the Original Bidder to give a Slam Invitation below the game level by bidding a new suit if his hand so warrants.

9. *The Jump to Four of Partner's Opening Bid in a Major Suit.* The response in all instances denies a high card holding of as much as 6, but at the same time indicates that Responder has sufficient trump support and enough distributional advantages to warrant a play for game.

10. *The Jump to Three of Partner's Opening Bid in*

a Minor Suit. This bid is forcing to game, and like the Jump to three in a major indicates both distributional and high card strength. It paves the way for a three-notrump bid.

11. *The Response of Two in a Higher Ranking Suit.* This unusual response has a special use in the Four Aces System and will be discussed in Part III.

12. *The Jump to Three of a Lower Ranking Suit.* This is a Slam Invitational Game Force and the bidding can never stop short of game.

These twelve responses cover the bidding possibilities of all normal hands.

CHAPTER VI

Choice of Responses to an Opening Bid of One in a Suit

LET us first consider the pass. In general we should rarely pass our partner's Opening one-bid, since he may need very little assistance from us to score a game. However, as it is absurd to tilt at windmills, we should pass with hands no stronger than the following:

♠ A x x   ♥ x x x x   ♦ x x x   ♣ x x x

♠ Q x   ♥ Q x x   ♦ x x x x   ♣ x x x x

It will be noted that each of these examples shows a balanced hand with a high card value less than the equivalent of three with two honors. Holding a King and a Queen or an Ace and a ten, we have a borderline holding and *may* still pass our partner's Opening bid of one of a suit.

With slightly stronger hands we must respond and should do so either by bidding one notrump, giving a single raise in partner's suit, or making a One-Over-One. Of these three bids the one notrump is the *least desirable,* since it immediately informs our opponents that our hand is weak, while at the same time it gives our partner no information as to where our meager high card strength is to be found. It should only be bid when we cannot avail ourselves of the other two responses. If our hand offers a choice between a One-Over-One response and a single raise in partner's suit a very close question is generally presented. The correct answer, however, can usually be found by adhering to the following rule:

If our hand is just strong enough for one response use the One-Over-One, intending to pass at our next opportunity unless partner in turn has forced. If our hand is clearly strong enough for two bids, again we first make the One-Over-One, holding in reserve our second bid. However, if we are in doubt as to whether our hand is worth one or two bids, we eliminate the uncertainty by giving an immediate raise in partner's suit. As this is not a Force, if our partner now rebids we are clearly able to make the second bid.

EXAMPLE HANDS SHOWING CHOICE BETWEEN THE ONE-OVER-ONE AND THE SINGLE RAISE

The following examples will illustrate this very important principle:

Partner bids one heart, and we hold:

♠ K Q x x   ♡ Q x x   ◊ x x x   ♣ x x x

High card value 4.

Bid one spade, intending to pass if partner's next bid is two spades, two hearts or one notrump.

♠ K Q J x   ♡ K Q x   ◊ x x x   ♣ x x x

High card value 6½.

With this hand we surely can afford to make two bids and so select one spade as our first response, intending to bid two hearts over partner's one notrump, or three hearts over partner's rebid of his suit.

♠ K Q x x   ♡ A x x   ◇ x x x   ♣ x x x

High card value 6.

Should we respond with one spade with this hand and partner then bid two hearts (a very probable second bid) we should be in a complete quandary as to whether to pass or to bid three hearts. We eliminate this future guess by giving an immediate Raise to two hearts.

The following hands are all too strong to pass partner's Opening bid. They offer a choice of one notrump, a One-Over-One response, or a Raise in suit.

♠ K x x   ♡ K x x   ◇ x x x x   ♣ x x x

High card value 4.

Respond with one notrump to a bid of any suit by partner.

♠ K x x x   ♡ x x x   ◇ K Q x   ♣ x x x

High card value 5.

If partner opens the bidding with a heart, a diamond, or a club, the inclination fostered by other systems is to respond with one notrump. However, a one-spade response does not prevent our partner from now bidding one notrump himself, and not only does it give partner a slightly better picture of our hand but at the same time it conceals our weakness from the opponents. Accordingly, under the Four Aces System the *minimum suit requirements for One-Over-One responses may be shaded at all times by the Responding Hand.* Should partner have opened with one spade we would of course immediately raise to two.

♠ A x x   ♡ K x x   ◇ Q J x   ♣ x x x x

High card value 6½.

It is particularly important to consider this hand as it gives a clear illustration of the Principle of Anticipation in connection with the first response. Assume that partner opens the bidding with one spade. Although we have three spades to the Ace, there is no suit we can ruff. Unless partner has abnormal distribution, we are not especially anxious to play this hand at game in spades. Therefore, the unthinking player would reply with one notrump. However, should we bid one notrump and our partner bid two spades, we can only guess what to do next. Two spades is obviously a safe contract, but should we bid three spades, we may be beyond our depth. On the other hand, failure to bid three spades may cause us to miss a game. This entire problem is eliminated if we anticipate this situation and make an immediate response of two spades. Even though partner has a minimum hand with a four-card spade suit, two spades should be as favorable a contract as one notrump; while if partner can afford to bid four spades, we are of course delighted; and if partner bids three spades, we can now bid three notrump, clearly indicating that our initial Raise was given with a balanced hand.

For similar reasons, we give an immediate Raise of partner's Opening bid of one in any other suit.

♠ K x x   ♡ x x x   ◇ K Q x x   ♣ x x x

High card value 5.

Over one club bid one diamond, since that bid does not shut out one notrump and keeps the bidding in the one zone, at the same time informing partner where our strength lies. Over one heart or one spade, bid one notrump; over one diamond, bid two diamonds.

♠ x x   ♡ A 10 x x   ◇ x x x x   ♣ x x x

High card value 3.

This hand is important as illustrating where we can make a One-Over-One response, but are not strong enough for one notrump. Should partner open with a diamond or a club, we bid one heart, intending of course to pass on the next round unless given an Absolute Force. If partner opens with one heart, we raise him to two, again, of course, having no intention of doing any more bidding. If he opens with one spade, we simply pass and do not invite trouble by a one-notrump response.

♠ Q J x x   ♡ x   ◇ K x x x   ♣ Q x x x

High card value 4½.

Our partner bids one spade. This hand is not strong enough distributionally or in high card strength to warrant a bid of more than two spades, so we reply with that bid, hoping our partner will bid again. If he opens with one diamond or one club, we respond with one spade rather than give an immediate Raise in partner's minor suit, because if partner also holds four spades it will be much easier to make ten tricks at spades than eleven tricks at diamonds or clubs. Secondly, we do not know how weak our partner's suit may be. Thirdly, we are prepared to return to partner's suit on our next bid. Over partner's one-heart bid we also bid one spade, but for a slightly different reason. Our holding is such that if partner opens with a heart, there is the possibility of a misfit. With such a hand the response should never be one notrump. The good player refrains from immediately bidding one notrump *to deny* partner's Opening suit bid. His notrump response generally shows some mild support for partner's suit. There are some slight exceptions to this generalization. For instance:

♠ x   ♡ Q J x x   ◇ K x x x   ♣ Q x x x

High card value 4½.

Answer partner's Opening heart bid with two hearts. Over one diamond or one club, bid one heart. Over one spade, bid one notrump in spite of and not because of the singleton small spade. We do not like to make this response, but on the other hand our holding is not strong enough to warrant a bid of two hearts over one spade and at the same time it is too strong to consider passing.

Let us next consider hands that are too strong for a one-notrump response but are not strong enough to warrant an immediate Game-Forcing bid. Hands in this class range from those containing slightly more than an Ace, a King, a Queen and a Jack, to hands with enormous high card values, but which suggest the danger of a misfit. Responses with these types of hands should be:

1. One-Over-One.
2. Two of a lower-ranking suit.
3. An immediate single Raise in partner's suit.

With a good hand the single Raise of partner's suit is the least desirable of these three possible responses. Unless partner holds a strong original bid he will pass and a game may be missed. The immediate single Raise should be given only when a response in a new suit cannot be found.

♠ K J 7 2   ♡ J 2   ◇ A Q 4 3   ♣ 10 x x

High card value 7.

With this hand we must prepare to make at least two bids and, therefore, should select a response that our partner will not pass, but which at the same time will permit him to drop the bidding below game. For instance, should he bid one club originally we respond with one spade, planning our future course of action as follows: If he replies to our one spade with one notrump, showing a minimum or near minimum, we next bid two notrump. This second-round two-notrump bid strongly invites partner to continue. However, unlike the immediate Jump to two notrump it is not an Absolute Force and he may pass with a bare minimum. If partner should bid two clubs over our one-spade we now bid two diamonds, hoping he will make an encouraging bid. If, however, he merely bids two spades or three clubs we pass, as partner's minimum bids clearly indicate that a game contract is not warranted. If over our one spade, partner bids two spades we now bid three diamonds, with the definite intention of carrying the bidding to game. (This bid of three diamonds is a Temporary Force.)

If our partner opens the bidding with one heart we also bid a spade, intending to develop the bidding in a manner similar to that following a one-club Opening. Over an Opening diamond bid our procedure is similar, with the one exception that if partner rebids diamonds we raise that suit.

Lastly let us consider our action in case our partner bids one spade. A two-spade bid on this hand would be inadequate, since a game seems likely. On the other hand, a three-spade bid would show more strength than the hand contains and if our partner opened a minimum, a game contract would be set. Accordingly, a middle course is followed. A two-diamond response is made which our partner may not pass. If he bids two spades our reply is three spades, strongly urging him to bid game, but still allowing him to pass with a minimum. If over two diamonds he bids two hearts, we also bid three spades, which, of course, he will not pass. If he bids two notrump over our two-diamond response, we bid three spades, in this instance a Forcing bid. The two-notrump has shown that the Opening bid was not a minimum, hence we must reach game. The three-spade bid offers a choice between a final contract of three notrump and four spades.

♠ x x   ♡ x x x   ◇ A x x   ♣ K Q x x x

High card value 6.

This hand has a high card value of only six, but with its good five-card club suit is too strong to consider a one-notrump response. Over partner's Opening one spade, the response should be two clubs. If partner replies with two spades we should pass, since we have no fit for spades, and he none for clubs, and the heart suit may be wide open against us. If, however, over our two clubs, he bids two hearts we should bid two notrump, encouraging him to bid three notrump but at the same time allowing him to sign off with three hearts if he has a two-suiter without much high card strength. Should he bid two diamonds, we should pass, as a game in diamonds appears to be very improbable and a notrump declaration might be dangerous because of the gap in hearts. Should he bid three clubs, we should gamble with three notrump, hoping that our partner has a heart stopper or that our opponents cannot run more than four tricks in that suit. Over partner's Opening one club, the correct bid is two clubs. If he can then bid two notrump we joyfully bid three. If he passes, the two-club contract cannot be defeated and there is little likelihood that there is a game in the hand.

♠ —   ♡ K J x   ◇ A Q 10 9 x x   ♣ A x x x

High card value 9½.

Partner bids a spade. Although we have a very fine hand, quite strong enough to justify an Opening bid in any position, the void in our partner's suit indicates a misfit and is a distinct danger signal—at least until we have more information about his hand. Therefore, although we intend to keep the bidding open until a game bid is reached we must "make haste slowly." With this in mind we bid only two diamonds, intending of course to bid and rebid until it can be determined which declaration is most likely to produce game. The information gained in reaching a game bid may even suggest that the hand should be played for a Slam. If partner opens the bidding with one heart our position is improved. There is now no danger of a misfit, and as Slam possibilities are at once suggested we make a Slam Invitational Game Force of three diamonds. Over a one-club Opening we should bid one diamond (a One-Over-One response).

♠ x x x   ♡ A Q x x   ◇ K 10 x   ♣ A x x

High card value 9.

This hand fulfills the high card and distributional requirements for a two-notrump response; nevertheless, if partner opens with one club or one diamond, we would choose the Exploratory one-heart, as we have no protection in spades. If partner opens with one heart, we are strong enough to give an immediate Raise to three; while if partner opens with one spade, we have one of those instances where our hand properly calls for an immediate Jump to two notrump. With a balanced hand and protection in all side suits, there is little to be gained by suggesting a game in hearts, and the two-notrump response is better. A further advantage of an immediate two-notrump bid with this hand lies in the fact that should we respond with two hearts and partner now bid two notrump, we would not be quite strong enough to warrant jeopardizing game by a bid of four notrump, but on the other hand, should we bid only three notrump we might be missing a Slam.

RAISES

The next type of hand to consider is the one that obviously calls for a Raise. The only question such hands present is how many Raises to give. An important factor is the trump strength. Four trumps are always desirable, and immediate Jump Raises should rarely be made with fewer. For a single Raise of a major suit bid, however, three to the Queen will frequently be sufficient trump strength, and, occasionally, even with such hands as the following:

♠ x x x   ♡ x   ◇ A x x x x   ♣ K x x x

we immediately raise a one-spade bid to two. Raises in a minor suit, however, should always show four trumps, and Jump Raises usually five, since partner may have bid on a three-card suit, and furthermore, we suggest playing hands at minor suit game contracts only when distribution makes it apparent that from the standpoint of safety and game possibilities the minor suit offers the best chance.

We come now to hands which present the question, "How many immediate Raises?" At this point we introduce a principle which has been used by experts for years, but which very few authors have ever advocated for general use or have incorporated into a complete bidding system. This is the Principle of Counting Losers.

COUNTING LOSERS

The Responding Hand counts losers by arbitrarily reading partner's bid as a minimum, such as four trumps to the A-K, the Ace of a side suit and the Queen of another, with perhaps a ten somewhere in the hand as well. If the holding of the Responding Hand makes impossible this particular minimum holding by partner, the conception of it is revised by the substitution, in his theoretical hand, of cards equivalent in value to those which our own holding shows it impossible for him to have. Thus if we hold either the Ace or the King of trumps, we mentally substitute equivalent cards to give the Opening bidder his proper minimum high card holding.

The following hands are examples of this process of counting losers when considering Jump Raises in partner's suit:

Partner bids one spade. We hold

♠ Q J x x   ♡ x   ◇ A x x x   ♣ K x x x

High card value 6½.

We set up at once a hypothetical minimum hand for our partner and picture this

♠ A K x x   ♡ A —   ◇ —   ♣ Q —

and additional low cards.

We now count losers. We see none in hearts, and none in spades. Probably he does not hold more than three diamonds or three clubs, so we count two losers in diamonds and two in clubs as the maximum. However, another Queen in his hand would probably save us a losing trick, but that slight additional value would not warrant his bidding over two spades. As success depends on so small a margin this hand is worth playing at game in spades. Our problem, then, is whether to raise to three or four spades. The answer is simple. As our high card holding is an Ace, a King, a Queen and a Jack, we must bid three spades, but should discourage any Slam Invitation by Bidder.

If partner's actual hand should include the Ace of clubs instead of the Ace of hearts our count of losers is still accurate, since we have reduced the club losers to a maximum of one to make up for the heart loser we now hold. Note also that if instead of the Ace of hearts partner holds the King and Queen, while we would have a loser in hearts, the favorable position of the adverse Ace (in front of the K-Q) might, by virtue of discards, reduce our losers in either clubs or diamonds to one instead of two. With this hand a holding of more than three clubs or more than three diamonds by partner would not increase the number of probable losers in either of these suits.

Suppose we hold

♠ A Q x x   ♡ A x x   ◊ A x x x   ♣ x x

High card value 10.

Again we at once visualize our partner's probable hand. Suppose he has the King of spades, the Ace of clubs, the King of diamonds and the King of hearts. That is a high card value of 9 and will represent a minimum bid. If the picture is a true representation we have no spade losers, and but one club, one diamond, and one heart loser. If our partner has good distribution and more than minimum high card strength, we wish to play the hand at a Slam, but if he has a minimum hand, bidding beyond four spades would be dangerous. Accordingly, we respond with a bid of three spades. This bid says: "Partner, I want to play this hand at game in spades. I have plenty of high cards. If your high card strength is substantially more than that required for a minimum bid, you may respond with some bid other than four spades. If you bid four spades, I shall pass."

> NOTE: *It should be observed in comparing this hand with the previous one that although the double Raise is given in both instances, the first hand is a minimum three-spade response, while the second is a maximum. With the first hand we will definitely discourage any Slam tries by partner, while with the second hand, if he does invite a Slam, we will bid it ourselves.*

Assume we hold

♠ K Q x x   ♡ A x   ◇ x x   ♣ K J 10 x x

High card value 8½.

Partner bids one club. Let us assume that he has the A-Q of that suit, the King of hearts and the spade or diamond Ace. Should he hold the Ace of spades we count no club loser, no spade loser, no heart loser, and two diamond losers, and know that the hand will play at five clubs with perfect safety, while the opponents might easily take five or six diamond tricks against a three-notrump contract. Should our partner hold three small spades, the King of hearts and the Ace-Queen of diamonds, we might lose two spade tricks and a diamond at five clubs, while we would have nine certain tricks if our partner played three notrump. Accordingly, with this hand we refrain from giving an immediate Jump Raise in clubs and bid one spade. If our partner now bids one notrump we respond with three clubs, which plainly says: "Partner, I could have bid three clubs originally, but I am not sure whether we should play this hand at notrump or at clubs. I am leaving the decision to you after first warning you that I am weak in diamonds or hearts."

Another example:

♠ x   ♡ A Q x x x x   ◇ Q x x x   ♣ x x

High card value 5.

Our partner has bid one heart. If he has only the King of hearts and the Ace and King of diamonds, game at four hearts is almost certain. On the other hand, if he holds the Ace and King of spades, the Ace and King of clubs, three diamonds to the King and the King of hearts, we still might be unable to make a Slam. Furthermore, although we can very probably make four hearts it is not unlikely that our opponents can defend very cheaply at spades. With this hand, therefore, a four-heart response is indicated, and if partner bids a Slam, he must do so entirely on his own responsibility.

♠ Q J x x x   ♡ x   ◇ x x   ♣ K J 10 x x

High card value 4.

Our partner opens with one spade. We jump to four.

THE IMMEDIATE TWO- AND THREE-NOTRUMP RESPONSES

The two-notrump response is made with a high card value of from $8\frac{1}{2}$ to $10\frac{1}{2}$, and, in addition, indicates a hand with preparation in all suits, including some mild support (at least J x or x x x) for partner's suit. It conveys the message: "Partner, I have heard your Opening bid and even though you have a minimum, I wish to play this hand at game; and unless for distributional reasons of your own you would much prefer a suit, I am suggest-

ing that three notrump is the best final contract. Furthermore, my hand is of such nature that an Exploratory Response by me would be of no help in future bidding."

The following hand:

♠ A J x   ♡ K x x   ◇ Q J x   ♣ K x x x

High card value 9.

is a proper two-notrump response to any Opening suit
bid, since we want to bid game, and are interested in a
Slam only if partner cares to bid it after the precise information we have given him.

Should we hold

♠ J x   ♡ A x x x   ◇ A J x x   ♣ K J x

High card value 9½.

and partner open with one spade, there is practically nothing to be gained by an Exploratory bid of two diamonds,
and we recommend a two-notrump response. If partner
opens with one heart, a three-heart bid is indicated. Over
an Opening bid of one-club, bid one diamond. An immediate Jump to two notrump is a bad bid. A player who
makes such a response, and later finds that a sure minor
suit game has been sacrificed, due to the fact that partner
also has no stopper in spades, has no right to complain
of bad luck—he has been guilty of bad bidding. Over an
Opening of one diamond, we may bid either three diamonds or one heart, and again two notrump would be bad.

The three-notrump response is similar to the two-notrump, except that it indicates a high card value of from
10½ to 12, and absolutely guarantees game. Furthermore, a hand which is a proper three-notrump bid over

one suit may warrant a stronger bid over another. For example:

♠ A x x   ♡ K x x x   ◇ K Q x   ♣ A J x

High card value 11½.

Should partner open with one club, diamond or spade, we will respond with three notrump. However, if he opens with one heart, our substantial high card values, combined with the fact that we hold four cards in his suit, would warrant stronger bidding. Accordingly, we would first force with three clubs, and then bid four hearts. In this instance, the Slam Invitational Game Force on a three-card suit is permissible, for irrespective of how high our partner raises clubs, we may always return to hearts at the same level.

JUMP RESPONSES IN A NEW SUIT

Jump Responses in a new suit always suggest the distinct possibility of a Slam and consequently we consider them under "Slam Bidding." We must point out that it is advisable to restrain the impulse to give an immediate Jump response in a new suit when our partner's declaration indicates a possible misfit.

THE QUALIFIED TEMPORARY FORCE

At this point we are prepared to introduce the Principle of the Qualified Temporary Force. This particular Force, which we have referred to in the Introduction, is strictly a common-sense measure, and may be defined in the following terms:

Rule: Any Temporary Forcing bid made by a player

who has passed originally is *qualified* by the
Limiting feature of the original pass.*

In other words, under the Four Aces System a player
who opens the bidding Third or Fourth Hand is *privileged* to pass his partner's Exploratory response in another suit. We wish to emphasize the word "privileged"
and to warn our readers that they should make use of the
permissive pass only when their Opening bid is either an
actual minimum or has been shaded for tactical reasons,
and then only when the hand is such that it contains no
logical rebid.

THE QUALIFIED GAME FORCE

We must now consider the following bids made by a
player who has passed, namely: The Jump bid to three of
partner's suit and the Jump bid to two notrump. These
bids are each a Qualified Game Force. Unlike the Qualified
Temporary Force, the Qualified Game Force must be
responded to unless the Third or Fourth Hand bidder has
shaded his Opening bid for tactical reasons.

Differing from the Qualified Force, a Jump bid in a
new suit by a player who has passed is absolutely forcing
to game.

Examples of how the Responding Hand considers these
various bids are as follows:

♠ K J 10 x ♡ x x ♢ A Q J x ♣ 10 x x

High card value 7.

If partner opens the bidding in third or fourth position
with one spade, a response of three spades is indicated.

* The original pass denies an Opening bid.

♠ A 10 x x   ♡ x x   ◇ A x x   ♣ K x x x

High card value 8.

If partner opens with a heart, a diamond or a club, our correct response is one spade, and not two notrump, even though we have passed originally. There is little danger attendant to this procedure because the Qualified Temporary Force is seldom passed and in this case if it is passed, the declaration is probably as favorable as any; while if partner is able to respond, we continue to develop the bidding in the most logical manner. However, if partner's Opening bid were one spade, we would consider it advisable to jump to three spades.

♠ K Q 10 x x x   ♡ K 10 x x   ◇ K x x   ♣ —

High card value 7.

If we pass this hand originally, and partner opens the bidding with one heart or one diamond, we should surely wish to reach a game declaration and therefore should make the Absolutely Forcing response of two spades. This Jump bid to two of a suit will be discussed in detail in Part III.

CHAPTER VII

Responses to Opening Bids of One Notrump

OUR partner's Opening one-notrump bid has told us:

1. That his high card value is 11½ to 13.
2. That his distribution is 5-3-3-2, 4-4-3-2 or 4-3-3-3.
3. That any doubleton in his hand includes either the King or the Ace.
4. That he expects to be able to take at least four or five tricks even though we have a bust.

Therefore, the Opening one-notrump bid says:

1. "I can play one notrump with reasonable safety, so do not rescue."
2. "I cannot make game unless you have either a high card value of at least five with three honors or distributional advantages to compensate. Therefore, if you lack such support you should not encourage me to attempt it."
3. "As I have given you definite information as to my minimum holding, I promise no rebid unless you force."
4. "On the other hand, since you are not required to bid I shall consider any response by you as showing certain definite values, and will probably rebid in

61

view of the game possibility which your response may show for our combined hands."

Since the Responding Hand has this precise knowledge at his disposal there is no need, after an Opening one notrump, for the so-called Exploratory bids. Hence all responses to the notrump opening are strength showing and are made either for the purpose of reaching game or for suggesting game, while occasionally allowing the bidding to stop at a safe part-score.

Tricks at notrump are taken by high cards and by established low cards of long suits. In estimating game possibilities at notrump, we must first consider the case where neither hand includes a five-card suit, in which event a combined high card value of $17\frac{1}{2}$ with 10 honors is sufficient to afford a reasonable chance for game. Possession of a *workable* five-card suit in either hand means one additional low-card trick and operates to reduce by almost a full point the necessary high-card requirements. A workable six-card suit indicates two or three low card tricks with the result that the high card value may be decreased by about $2\frac{1}{2}$ points. Of course, when high card requirements are reduced on account of the presence of workable suits, care must be taken to guard against the possibility that our opponents can set up and run a suit of their own.

It is interesting to note that a combined high card holding of $22\frac{1}{2}$, without the assistance of any long suit, will offer better than an even chance for six notrump.

NORMAL RESPONSES TO AN OPENING ONE-NOTRUMP BID

The normal responses to an Opening one-notrump bid are as follows:

1. *The Pass,* made with a high card value of less than 5 with three honors, unless Responder holds a strong suit or a freakish hand.

2. *The Bid of Two of a Minor Suit.* This is the only response to an Opening bid of one notrump which in any manner invites a pass. The reason why this bid invites a pass is logical and is due to the fact that generally it is undesirable after an Opening one-notrump bid to try for game in a minor suit unless we wish to disclose Slam possibilities. (See 7.) Therefore, after a one-notrump bid, having a fair hand with a five- or six-card minor suit, we should respond with two notrump; having a good hand, three notrump. Accordingly, the response of two in a minor suit tells partner that we have a hand that offers a slight possibility of game, and that it is not strong enough to invite game by bidding two no-trump.

3. *The Bid of Two of a Major Suit.* This bid invites a pass only if partner has an absolute minimum or shaded one-notrump bid. Otherwise, we expect him to rebid notrump or raise our suit.

4. *The Two-Notrump Response.* This indicates a hand with a minimum high card value of 5, including three honors, and a maximum high card value of 7 with three honors. It is a near Force and should be passed by partner only if his Opening one no-trump was shaded.

5. *The Three-Notrump Response.* This indicates a hand with a minimum high card value of 7 and a maximum high card value of 9 with four honors. It guarantees game, but invites a Slam only if part-

ner has *more than the maximum one-notrump strength.*

NOTE: *The high card holdings generally necessary to make the two- and three-notrump responses can be somewhat reduced if the Responding Hand includes a workable five-card suit, and substantially reduced if the hand includes a good six-card suit.*

6. *The Bid of Three in a Major Suit.* This is made merely to invite partner to choose between game at notrump and the suit, or, with a stronger hand, as the first bid on the way to a Slam.

7. *The Bid of Three in a Minor Suit.* This bid in all cases suggests Slam possibilities since with a strong minor suit and a hand we desire to play at game only, we should simply bid two or three notrump.

8. *The Bid of Four in a Major Suit.* This bid is usually made with at least a seven-card suit and denies outside strength. It indicates a hand that should produce a major suit game and that lack of re-entries and high cards make notrump play undesirable. Unlike other jumps to game it is a definite sign-off, following which no original one-notrump hand should be rebid.

EXAMPLE HANDS OF NORMAL RESPONSES TO AN OPENING ONE-NOTRUMP BID

The following illustrations are given to indicate the proper responses to a one-notrump opening:

♠ x   ♡ x x x   ◇ x x x x x x   ♣ x x x

High card value o.

Pass. Do not rescue unless one notrump has been doubled.

♠ K x x   ♡ K x x   ◇ x x x x   ♣ x x x

High card value 4.

Pass. Due to the limiting feature of partner's Opening notrump, we realize that even though there might be a possible play for game the chances of success would be extremely remote—not good enough to compensate for the almost sure loss that would be incurred should we increase the contract.

♠ x x   ♡ x x   ◇ A x x x x x   ♣ Q x x

High card value 4.

Bid two diamonds. With a minimum, partner will pass. If, however, he shows additional values by bidding two notrump we can now well afford to raise to three.

♠ x x   ♡ x x   ◇ A Q x x x x   ♣ x x x

High card value 4.

This hand is the same in high card strength and distribution as in the preceding example, but due to the fact that the diamond suit is so strong and that partner's original one-notrump bid guarantees a minimum of King and one diamond, or three small, we wish to play the hand at game, and therefore respond with two notrump.

♠ A x x   ♡ K x x   ◇ x x x x   ♣ x x x

High card value 5.

Pass. This hand with but two honors and no five-card suit does not warrant a Raise.

♠ K 10 x x x   ♡ A x   ◇ 10 x x   ♣ x x x

High card value 5.

This hand fits the minimum requirements for a two-no-trump response, but we recommend the more conservative bid of two spades. If our partner now bids either two no-trump or three spades, we bid three notrump. If the diamond and spade suits were reversed, the response should be two notrump rather than two diamonds.

♠ A x x   ♡ K x x   ◇ K x x   ♣ Q x x x

High card value 8.

Bid three notrump. We are certain of game, but there is practically no possibility of a Slam.

♠ Q J x x x x   ♡ A x   ◇ x x   ♣ x x

High card value 4½.

Bid four spades. This hand should surely produce game in spades after partner's opening notrump, and obviously we are not interested in a Slam.

♠ x x   ♡ A x   ◇ Q J x x x x   ♣ x x

High card value 4½.

This is the same hand as the preceding example, except that the spade and diamond suits are reversed. The hand is not strong enough for three diamonds, but on the other hand it is too strong for two diamonds; we bid two notrump, since partner almost certainly holds either the King or the Ace of diamonds and there should be a very good play for game at notrump.

♠ K x   ♡ A x   ◇ A Q x x x x   ♣ x x

High card value 9.

With the strong seven-card diamond suit we visualize a certain Slam after partner's Opening notrump even though we know that our opponents will hold some of the high cards. Furthermore, we even see possibilities of a Grand Slam and first respond with three diamonds, intending to bid six notrump at our next opportunity.

♠ K x   ♡ K Q J x x   ◇ Q x x   ♣ A x x

High card value 9½.

With the advantage of the five-card heart suit, plus the high card value, we visualize a good play for six, even though partner holds a minimum notrump. On the other hand, we do not care to invite seven and, furthermore, if he has shaded the requirements for an Opening notrump, six might be in danger. With our balanced distribution there is no point in playing the hand at hearts, so we make the unusual immediate response of five notrump, which implies: "Partner, please bid six, unless you have shaded the requirements for your one notrump, but do not bid seven."

♠ K x x   ♡ K Q x x   ◇ K x x   ♣ A x x

High card value 10.

This hand contains more high card strength than the fore-going example, but it has one less heart and is, therefore, by no means so desirable. On the other hand, there are Slam possibilities which we show by the immediate response of four notrump which says: "Partner, if you have a *maximum* notrump bid more."

The reader in his study of these examples will have noted the great value we assign to a long suit when held opposite an Opening notrump. The reason for this is that since partner's Opening notrump has shown strength in all suits we always anticipate that the low cards in our long suit will take tricks.

♠ K J 10 x x x x   ♡ x   ◇ x x   ♣ x x x

High card value 2½.

We surely wish to play this hand at game, but just as surely do not wish to reach a Slam contract. An immediate four-spade response is indicated.

♠ K x x   ♡ x x   ◇ x x x x   ♣ A 10 x x

High card value 5 with 3 honors.

Although this hand warrants a minimum two-notrump response, we recommend two clubs because we do not care to invite game if partner's Opening notrump is a minimum.

REBIDS BY THE OPENING ONE-NOTRUMP BIDDER

This is one of the simplest problems in Contract, but only when properly handled.

The following rules give the correct procedure for the Original Bidder, after he has opened with one notrump.

1. Bid three notrump over a two-notrump response, unless the one-notrump bid was shaded.
2. In general, make some further bid over a response of two of a major suit.
3. With a minimum or near-minimum notrump, pass a response of two in a minor suit.
4. With a maximum notrump, invite a Slam over a Forcing response.
5. *Pass a three-notrump response unless holding more than the maximum requirement for an opening one-notrump bid.*

CHAPTER VIII

Résumé of Responses

THE Four Aces Theory of Responses, as shown in the preceding chapters, is in marked contrast to that advanced in any other book or advocated by any other authority. We believe, however, that the success we have attained in tournament competition and rubber play is very largely due to our Theory of Responses and particularly to our selection of the initial response.

Certain of the principles are so important and revolutionary that they are, for emphasis, repeated below:

1. The principle that one notrump should not be made as the first response when any other is properly available. Consider the following hand:

♠ 10 9 x x x   ♡ A x   ◇ Q x x   ♣ x x x

High card value 4.

Partner opens the bidding with one heart, one diamond or one club. Our best response is one spade. Nevertheless, a great many Bridge players would respond with one notrump. This is due to their mistaken conception that any response other than one notrump is strength-showing. Let us repeat that under our system the One-Over-One is a neutral response and may, in extreme cases, be made with a hand that is too weak even for a one notrump response, such as:

♠ A x x x x x   ♡ x x   ◇ x x x   ♣ x x

which we advocate as a definite one-spade response to an Opening bid in any other suit.

To us the decision with the above hands would not seem close. However, let us consider the following:

♠ K J x x   ♡ x x x   ◇ K x x   ♣ x x x

High card value 4½.

If partner opens with one heart, one diamond or one club about ninety percent of the Bridge players in the country would respond with one notrump. A very few would pass. The remaining, including ourselves, would bid one spade, and we strongly recommend the bid since it gives so much better information to partner than would one notrump or a pass.

We also dislike the two-notrump response but to a somewhat lesser degree. For instance, consider the following hand:

♠ x x x   ♡ x x   ◇ A K x x   ♣ A Q x x

High card value 9.

Partner bids one spade. With this hand most Bridge players respond with two notrump and then complain bitterly of their bad luck when partner bids three and an unkind but alert opponent opens a heart through partner's King and defeats the contract. While this hand is strong enough in high cards for a two-notrump response, we are not particularly anxious to become declarer on account of the worthless doubleton in hearts and select the Temporary

Forcing bid of two diamonds over partner's one spade bid hoping he will bid the notrump. However, should he bid two hearts we can safely bid two notrump. Should he bid two spades, showing a rebiddable spade suit, we would bid four spades. Should partner bid three diamonds over our two diamonds we would finally be forced to bid three notrump, but even then should he have an unbalanced hand he would not let us play notrump.

Another bad bid that we find prevalent is the *unsound* Jump Raise. For instance, our partner bids one diamond. We hold

♠ A x x ♡ K x x ◊ Q x x x x ♣ x x

High card value 6.

Many players promptly but unwisely jump to three. This is a distinct overbid. If he now bids three notrump we naturally pass. It is unlikely that our combined hands can produce nine tricks. Why not give partner a chance to use his own judgment by bidding two diamonds? Now if he bids again we are quite certain of game, while if he does not rebid we should obtain a partial score.

The above hand is an introduction to a résumé of the use of Jump Raises. Under the Four Aces System the Jump to either three or four of partner's suit indicates in each case approximately the same supporting strength, and of course adequate trumps. The difference lies mainly in the matter of flexibility—the jump to four indicates that the raise is based principally on distribution, while the jump to three shows a fairly substantial high card holding in addition to trump support. The reader should bear in mind that both bids suggest the same final contract, namely game in the suit bid, and, therefore, should we jump our partner's suit bid to three and he then merely rebid to four, we have no excuse for inviting a Slam and such bidding as

Bidder	Responder
1 ♠	3 ♠
4 ♠	5 ♠

would be inexcusable. A hand strong enough to warrant such bidding is also strong enough to justify a Slam Invitational Game Force in a new suit.

SUMMARY

In responding to Opening bids of one notrump, the reader should bear in mind the following principles:

The first point is that there is no necessity for rescue bids. Therefore, any response to one notrump is definitely constructive. The second point is that a response of two in a minor, while constructive, invites the original bidder to pass with a minimum or near-minimum notrump, and may frequently show a hand just strong enough, or not quite strong enough, for a two-notrump response, such as

♠ x x x   ♡ J x x   ◇ A x x   ♣ Q J x x

High card value 5 with 4 honors.

This is not a particularly good hand and one with which we do not wish to reach a game bid if partner has but a minimum notrump. We tell him so by bidding two clubs.

If we open the bidding with a maximum one notrump, representing a high card value of 13, and partner passes with 4½, we have lost a good opportunity of scoring game. Conversely, if we open the bidding with a minimum notrump and partner raises to two with a high card value of 5, we will, of course, bid three and will then be in the uncomfortable position of trying to make three notrump with a high card value of only 16½. In most instances we overcome these uncertainties by the use of the two-club or two-diamond response which we make in both cases with hands on the borderline between a pass and a bid. Now if partner's original notrump is a minimum he passes our Chance-giving response. If his bid is a maximum he jumps to three notrump, while with an intermediate hand he bids two notrump, allowing us to decide whether or not to continue.

Examples of hands warranting this bid are:

♠ A x x   ♡ J x x   ◊ 10 x x   ♣ Q x x x

High card value 4½ with 4 honors.

Over partner's Opening notrump a response of two clubs will enable him intelligently to decide whether to bid two or three notrump.

♠ A x x   ♡ Q x x   ◊ x x x   ♣ Q 10 x x

High card value 5 with 4 honors.

While this hand, of course, warrants a two-notrump response, the somewhat weaker bid of two clubs may be made with the intention of bidding three notrump if partner bids two.

Other points the reader should bear in mind are:

1. After an Opening suit bid an immediate two- or three-notrump response always shows some support in partner's suit—a minimum of Jack and one.

2. That we may give an immediate Single Raise of partner's major suit bid on a trump holding as weak as three small when our hand contains certain values but no

satisfactory bid. A Jump Raise, however, should never be made without more adequate help in trumps.

3. That the proper use of the Exploratory Response in a new suit enables us to avoid embarrassing problems.

CHAPTER IX

Theory of the Development of the Bidding

THUS far we have discussed five distinct Opening bids and the responses thereto. Combinations of these lead to a great number of different situations which must be considered in connection with the development of the bidding. Naturally, it is impossible to treat each of these situations separately. However, having followed the Principle of Anticipation in the Opening bid and in the first response, the next and subsequent responses will follow so logically and simply that experience will suffice to show the reader how we develop the bidding toward a Slam, game or *safe* partial score contract.

The reader will note that the word "safe" relates to partial score contracts only. Success in making a game contract is rewarded with a substantial bonus. Accordingly, it is good tactics to try for game with any combination of cards which promises a reasonable play, and is safe against the possibility of a severe penalty.

On the other hand, when we stop at a partial score, we receive no bonus * for fulfilling our contract, and should endeavor to make such contracts as safe as possible.

This introduces our first theoretical principle in connection with partial score contracts, namely, that of the Stop-

* Except the value the partial score may assume in succeeding hands.

75

ping Place. By far the most desirable Stopping Place is two of a suit or one notrump. One of a suit would be equally satisfactory were it not that experience has shown that a score of 40 or 60 below the line is worth substantially more than a score of 20 or 30. Three of a minor suit is a fair Stopping Place since we are still two tricks below game. Higher bids, namely, two notrump, three of a major, or four of a minor bring us to within one trick of game. If we have reached a contract of one trick less than game by precise and logical bidding methods, we should realize that with good luck we can make game. We stop one trick below game only when we believe our contract is already too high.

The second principle deals with the development of the bidding when one player bids two suits and is known as the *Rule of Return*. When a player holds two suits which he wishes to bid, he must prepare for the sequence of bidding by properly selecting the suit to bid first. When your partner bids two suits, the probabilities are that his first suit is at least as strong as his second, although there are instances when he bids the weaker first. Therefore, having the same number of cards in each of his suits, it is essential that you at least *return* from his second to his first suit. In making this *return* you must bear in mind that you are not showing any additional values or strength, but are merely telling your partner that you are as well prepared for his first suit as for his second. He should realize this, and must not assume that your *return* has shown any additional values.

Let us consider the hand with two biddable suits. The bid of the second suit is what we call a *Shift*, of which there are two types, namely, the *Level Shift* and the *Skip Level Shift*. For example, suppose we bid one spade, partner two clubs, and we bid two hearts; our two-heart bid is a *Level Shift* since it allows a *Return* to spades at the same level. Also, one club by us, one heart by partner, one spade by us is a Level Shift since even though it invites a return at a higher level, nevertheless, that is the lowest level at which we could have rebid clubs. However, one diamond by us, two clubs by partner, two hearts by us, is a Skip Level Shift, because it invites a return to diamonds at a higher level—that of three—when we could have rebid at two.

In showing two suits a player should bear in mind that whereas the Level Shift does not necessarily show additional values, the Skip Level Shift must always be read as a strength-showing bid. It indicates a hand almost as strong as one with which we jump, thus: One spade, two hearts, three diamonds skips a level and invites a *Return* to three spades and is almost as strong as: One spade, two hearts, three spades. In choosing which of two suits to bid first, the good player *always anticipates his partner's response,* and with a weak hand so selects his first bid that he *will not be compelled* to make a Skip Level Shift. Furthermore, when his bid of a second suit constitutes a *Level Shift* only, his partner should *not rely* on him for more than four cards in either. When he gives a Skip Level Shift, partner should read the first suit as being of five cards. Therefore, if we decide to make a Skip Level Shift with two four-card suits, we should have tremendous high card strength to compensate.

SIGN-OFFS

The final principle to be considered is that of the *Sign-off*. The best and only complete Sign-off is the pass. However, there are frequent instances when you realize that by passing you would be stopping at an obviously unsatisfactory contract, whereas a further bid by you, if passed by partner, would improve matters. If such further bid can be read as a Sign-off, it is safe for you to make it.

The absolute definition of what are and are not Sign-offs is almost impossible; nevertheless, there are many sequences of bidding which should give warning of weakness. For instance, any time when we repeatedly rebid one suit in minimums. The first rebid may or may not be a Sign-off; the second rebid must be. Similarly, any time a player makes a simple Return, he may be signing off.

To summarize the preceding points:

1. *The Stopping Place.* Proper bidding aims at a *safe* part-score, a game or a Slam. Safe part-scores are those of two tricks less than game, and we should endeavor to avoid stopping at one trick below game.

2. *The Return.* When our partner bids two suits he is inviting us to return to his first suit if our support is as good as in the second suit, and such Return is not a Raise.

3. *The Level Shift.* The Level Shift occurs when our bid of a second suit invites a return to our first suit at the lowest level at which we, ourselves, could have rebid it. It does not necessarily indicate any more strength than a simple rebid.

4. *The Skip Level Shift.* The Skip Level Shift occurs when our bid of a second suit invites a return to our first suit at a higher level than we, ourselves, could have made a simple rebid. It indicates considerable values in addition to those which would be shown by a simple rebid.

5. *The Sign-off.* Any bid which warns partner that we do not desire any further bid by him.

As successful development of the bidding also depends in a great measure on a thorough understanding of what constitutes a Force, an Invitational bid, or a Sign-off, we give a complete summary of such bids:

Game Forces

1. Any Opening bid of two of a suit.
2. Any Jump bid by the partner of the original bidder.
3. Any Jump bid in a new suit by the original bidder.

Temporary Forces

4. Any bid of one of a suit over partner's bid of one of a suit (the One-Over-One).
5. Any bid by Responding Hand of two of a suit over an Opening bid of one of a higher ranking suit.
6. Any Skip Level Shift by Responding Hand.
7. Any bid of a new suit after some suit has been fitted.

Qualified Game Forces

8. Any Jump bid in notrump or in a previously bid suit by the Original Bidder.

Invitational Bids

9. Any bid of one less than game unless clearly a sign-off.
10. Any Skip Level Shift by the Original Bidder.
11. Any bid of a new suit by the Responding Hand.
12. An Opening bid of one of a suit or of two notrump.

Sign-offs

There is no definite rule, but the following bids may be Sign-offs:

1. A Return.

2. Repeated minimum rebids of the same suit. (These probably are Sign-offs.)

3. The introduction of a new suit when obviously it is mentioned only in a desperate effort to find a fit.

The Game Force No. 2 and Temporary Forces 4 and 5, as listed above, may be qualified by an original pass. The reader should also bear in mind that if a Qualified Game Force receives a response the qualified feature is removed and the bidding must continue to game.

ILLUSTRATIONS OF FORCES, SIGN-OFFS, ETC.

Illustrations of the above bids are:

Bidder	Responder
1 ♠	2 ♦ [1]
3 ♠ [2]	

[1] A Temporary Force.

[2] A Qualified Game Force. The three-spade bidder does not expect partner to pass. But if partner holds

♠ —   ♡ x x x   ♦ K J 10 x x x   ♣ x x x x

High card value 2½.

he should pass, since his bid of two diamonds was not made as a constructive bid.

Bidder	Responder
1 ♦	1 ♠ [1]
3 ♠ [2]	

[1] A Temporary Force.

[2] A Qualified Force, since the three-spade bidder does not expect his partner to pass. However, if Responder holds

♠ K 10 x x   ♡ J x x x   ◇ x   ♣ x x x x

High card value 2½.

he should pass because in order for there to be any reasonable play for game, bidder should have been able to make a stronger bid than three spades.

Bidder	Responder
1 ♠	2 ◇ [1]
2 ♠ [2]	3 ♣ [3]

[1] A Temporary Force.
[2] Responding to the Temporary Force.
[3] An Invitational bid. Original bidder, holding

♠ A K x x x   ♡ K x x   ◇ x x   ♣ Q x x

High card value 8.

should pass, since his Opening bid is borderline, and since game appears unlikely at either notrump or clubs.

Bidder	Responder
1 ♠	2 ♣ [1]
2 ♠ [2]	3 ◇ [3]

[1] A Temporary Force.
[2] Responding to the Temporary Force.
[3] A Skip Level Shift continuing the Temporary Force. Irrespective of what original bidder holds, he must bid again.

Bidder	Responder
1 ♠	2 ♠ [1]
2 N T [2]	3 ◇ [3]

[1] A single Raise in suit—a Limiting response.

[2] A Temporary Force, inviting partner at least to go back to three spades.

[3] Another Temporary Force, since the Responding Hand has bid a new suit after raising spades and obviously has no intention of playing diamonds. He is merely telling the original bidder that if he wants to bid three notrump he can count on stoppers in spades and diamonds, but must beware of clubs and hearts.

Bidder	Responder
1 ♠	2 ♠
3 ♠ [1]	

[1] An Invitational bid, obviously inviting Responder to bid four.

Bidder	Responder
1 ♠	2 ♡ [1]
2 N T [2]	3 ♡ [3]

[1] A Temporary Force.

[2] An invitation, showing substantial additional values.

[3] A sign-off, which says: "Partner, you not only opened the bidding but followed with a strong game invitation. Furthermore, your two notrump has shown some strength in hearts. Nevertheless, I do not care to play notrump and I cannot afford to bid four hearts myself."

Bidder	Responder
1 ♠	2 ♡ [1]
2 ♠ [2]	3 ♡ [3]

[1] A Temporary Force.

[2] Responding to the Temporary Force and showing a rebiddable spade suit.

[3] Showing a good heart suit. It may be read as a *partial* Sign-off, but the original bidder may continue.

Bidder	Responder
1 ♠	1 N T [1]
2 ♠ [2]	2 N T [3]
3 ♡ [4]	

[1] A weak limiting response.

[2] Either indicates a hand unsuitable for notrump play or shows additional values.

[3] Shows the one-notrump was a maximum.

[4] A Sign-off since if the original bidder had desired to show hearts for a possible game in that suit he would have done so on the preceding round. It merely says: "Partner, notrump is definitely unsuitable. My spade suit is not strong enough to bid a third time. Perhaps hearts is the best spot. If not return to spades at this level."

Bidder	Responder
1 ♡	1 N T [1]

[1] A weak, limiting response.

The following are examples of shifts:

Bidder	Responder
1 ♣	1 ♡
1 ♠ [1]	

[1] A Level Shift inviting a return to two clubs and at the same time not shutting out a bid of one notrump. Hence it does not *necessarily* indicate any greater strength than a bid of one notrump or two clubs.

Bidder	Responder
1 ♠	1 N T
2 ♡ [1]	

[1] A Level Shift inviting a return to two spades, and hence not *necessarily* indicating any greater strength than a bid of two spades.

Bidder	Responder
1 ♢	2 ♣
2 ♠ [1]	

[1] A Skip Level Shift shutting out the return to two diamonds and hence indicating practically as much strength as a Jump to three diamonds.

Bidder	Responder
1 ♠	2 ♡
3 ♢ [1]	

[1] A Skip Level Shift not only shutting out two spades but also immediately taking the bidding past the level of two and hence indicating a very good hand.

Due to the fact that the successive steps in scientific bidding should mesh as precisely as gears and are based at times on subtle inferences, we deemed it necessary under Responses frequently to indicate the course of action of the Responding Hand. In the next chapter we shall consider the development of the bidding principally from the viewpoint of the Opening bidder but, in explaining his rebids, the proper course of the Responding Hand will be indicated to a considerable extent.

CHAPTER X

Development of the Bidding after an Opening Bid of One of a Suit

WE HAVE previously discussed the different types of responses to the Opening bid of one of a suit. Our partner's response will have been either Limiting, Exploratory Game Forcing, or Slam Invitational. If Limiting, it will, in addition, show either weakness (one notrump or single Raise in suit), or strength (a Jump bid in notrump or a Jump Raise in suit).* If Exploratory it will be either neutral (One-Over-One) or strong (two of a lower ranking suit). Slam Invitational responses will be discussed under Slam Bidding.

Assuming we have opened the bidding with a balanced pattern (a hand with a distribution of 4-3-3-3, 4-4-3-2 or 5-3-3-2) and partner responds with one notrump, we should be able immediately to decide:

1. That our combined hands offer no play for game.

2. That our combined hands offer a very slight possibility of game.

3. That our combined hands will probably offer a play for game.

4. That our combined hands will make game.

* As previously explained, Responder, by means of an immediate Jump in notrump or partner's suit even though it may be forcing, nevertheless sets certain definite limits on the strength of his hand.

The decision is based entirely on the Principle of Limits and the combination of our high card values with the maximum and minimum values (3 to 6½) that partner's one-notrump response has shown. If our hand has a value of 10 or less we should abandon the thought of game and simply allow one notrump to be played. If we have 10½ or 11, we should also pass even though we might conceivably miss game. With 11½ to 13 a problem is presented, since if partner has a maximum one-notrump we should make game, while if he has a minimum response, two notrump would be unsafe. With such a hand, however, we generally avoid this awkward situation *by bidding one notrump* originally. With more than 13, we can afford to bid either two or three notrump after partner's one-notrump response.

When we open with an unbalanced hand and partner responds with one notrump, our problem is somewhat different. With a minimum or near-minimum hand, we may realize that one notrump is an undesirable contract and therefore rebid our suit or make a Level Shift, hoping that our second bid will not encourage partner unduly.

When partner's response is a single Raise in our suit, again, by the Principle of Limits, we are able to tell which hands clearly call for a pass and which call for a Jump to game. With intermediate hands we may invite further action by bidding three of our suit, or two notrump.

EXAMPLES OF DEVELOPMENT OF BIDDING

The following hands give specific instances of how we handle these problems:

♠ A 3 2   ♡ A 3 2   ◊ A 7 6 5 2   ♣ 4 2

High card value 9.

As this is an absolute minimum diamond bid a response of either one notrump or two diamonds should be passed.

♠ A K 10 9 6 5   ♡ A Q 6   ◊ 3 2   ♣ 3 2

High card value 9.

Although borderline in high card strength this is a very fine hand. If partner's response is one notrump we rebid spades to two. If he now bids two notrump, showing that his first bid was a maximum, we immediately jump to four spades. If partner's first response is two spades, we must take further action, since there is great likelihood that our combined hands will produce game, particularly if he holds two or three key cards. On the other hand, if his two-spade response is a minimum, a bid of even three spades might be set one trick. However, the good chance of making game outweighs the possibilities of a set and we bid three spades as a very strong invitation to partner to bid four.

♠ A J 8 7 2   ♡ A K 2   ◊ 6 5 4   ♣ 7 3

High card value 8½.

With this hand a one-notrump or two-spade response by partner suggests no game possibilities and either bid should be passed.

♠ 6 2   ♡ A K 6 4 3 2   ◊ A 2   ♣ 5 4 3

High card value 8.

If partner responds to one heart with one notrump we bid two hearts, not as an invitation to game but rather as a warning against notrump. If partner now bids again we bid three hearts, which is obviously a Sign-off. It partner's response is two hearts this hand calls for a pass.

♠ A K x x x   ♡ A x x   ◇ K x x   ♣ x x

High card value 10.

Pass a one-notrump response. Bid three spades over a two-spade response.

♠ A   ♡ K Q J x x x   ◇ A x x   ♣ K x x

High card value 11½.

As this hand is very powerful, over a one-notrump response we would bid three hearts, intending subsequently to bid four. If the response is two hearts, we immediately bid four.

♠ A Q 10 x x x   ♡ A x x x   ◇ x x   ♣ x

High card value 7.

Because of its strong distributional value this hand is a sound one-spade bid. If partner responds with two spades we should bid three to invite game. On the other hand, over a discouraging one-notrump response we should merely bid two spades, intending to rebid our spade suit as a Sign-off thereafter.

♠ A x   ♡ A x   ◇ K 10 x x x x   ♣ K x x

High card value 10.

We bid one diamond. In spite of its lack of solidity this is a good hand, particularly if partner can fit our six-card diamond suit. If he responds with one notrump we bid two diamonds, and if he then bids two notrump, we make the slightly sporting bid of three notrump. If his initial response is two diamonds we strongly invite game by bidding two notrump.

♠ A x ♡ A Q x x x ◇ A Q x ♣ x x x

High card value 11.

If partner responds to one heart with one notrump there is a slight possibility of game and we bid two hearts, intending to contract for game in notrump if he bids again. If partner's response is two hearts we must also take further action, which we do by bidding two notrump. If he can now bid three notrump we are delighted. If he has a strong heart Raise and jumps to four hearts we are also content; while if he merely bids three hearts, we recognize that he is signing off and pass.

The next class of responses are the stronger Limiting bids such as Jump Raises in partner's suit and Jump bids in notrump. Let us consider our procedure with the same nine hands if partner makes one of these stronger Limiting responses.

♠ A 3 2 ♡ A 3 2 ◇ A 7 6 5 2 ♣ 4 2

High card value 9.

Bid one diamond.
Over a two-notrump or three-diamond response we bid three notrump. Over a three-notrump response we pass.

♠ A K 10 9 6 5 ♡ A Q 6 ◇ 3 2 ♣ 3 2

High card value 9.

Bid one spade.
If partner's response is three spades, we bid four; if four spades, we pass. If partner's response is two notrump, we bid three spades in order to let him choose the final game contract. If partner's first response is three notrump, we take positive Slam action by bidding five spades.

♠ A J 8 7 2   ♡ A K 2   ◇ 6 5 4   ♣ 7 3

High card value 8½.

Having bid one spade we raise partner's three-spade response to four, and pass his four-spade bid. Similarly, we
raise his two-notrump to three, and pass his three-notrump.

♠ 6 2   ♡ A K 6 4 3 2   ◇ A 2   ♣ 5 4 3

High card value 8.

Having bid one heart we raise partner's three-heart response to four, and pass if he bids four hearts. Over two-
notrump we bid three hearts, leaving the choice between
four hearts and three notrump to him. Over a three-notrump bid we see slight Slam possibilities and bid four
hearts, thereby informing partner that our length in that
suit is our only additional value.

♠ A K x x x   ♡ A x x   ◇ K x x   ♣ x x

High card value 10.

Bid one spade.
Over a three-spade response we bid four spades; over
four spades we pass. Over a two-notrump bid we bid three
notrump. We should raise a three-notrump response to
four notrump, since even though the combined hands show
a maximum high card value of only 22 (10 + 12), our
fifth spade may insure the Slam.*

♠ A   ♡ K Q J x x x   ◇ A x x   ♣ K x x

High card value 11½.

---

* It was previously mentioned that a combined high card value of 22½
would indicate a good play for a Slam in notrump, even though neither
partner held a five-card suit.

Bid one heart.

After any Jump response by partner we cannot afford to let the bidding die short of a Slam. Our procedure with this hand will be shown in the chapters on Slam bidding.

♠ A Q 10 x x x   ♡ A x x x   ◇ x x   ♣ x

High card value 7.

Bid one spade.

With this hand after a three-spade response we bid four, while we pass a four-spade response. Over a two-notrump response we bid three spades, intending subsequently to bid four spades if partner then bids three notrump. Over a three-notrump response we bid four spades, placing the responsibility for further action on our partner.

♠ A x   ♡ A x   ◇ K 10 x x x x   ♣ K x x

High card value 10.

Bid one diamond.

With this hand we bid three notrump over a two-notrump response, while over three notrump we invite a Slam by a bid of four notrump. If partner responds with three diamonds, we have one of those problems which can be solved only by a look at partner's hand—no system can help us. For instance, four diamonds to the Ace will undoubtedly be as valuable trump support as four to the Ace-Queen-Jack; three clubs to the Ace and the King-small of hearts will be one trick less valuable than the Ace-small of clubs and three hearts to the King. The best we can do is to make a safe bid of three notrump.

♠ A x   ♡ A Q x x x   ◇ A Q x   ♣ x x x

High card value 11.

Having bid one heart, we raise a two-notrump response to three, or pass a four-heart response. The three-heart and three-notrump responses will be considered under Slam bidding.

DEVELOPMENT OF BIDDING AFTER AN EXPLORATORY RESPONSE

The third class of responses comprises the Exploratory bids, or bids of a new suit. It must be borne in mind that these Exploratory Responses are of two classes: The One-Over-One which gives practically no information as to the strength of the Responding Hand, and the bid of two in a lower-ranking suit which shows that the Responding Hand has some definite values. The same hands are used to illustrate:

♠ A 3 2   ♡ A 3 2   ◊ A 7 6 5 2   ♣ 4 2

High card value 9.

If partner responds to one diamond with either one heart or one spade, we are in a slightly unsatisfactory position, since we do not care to bid one notrump with the worthless doubleton in clubs, and accordingly must raise his suit with three trumps. Having now indicated slightly more strength than we actually have, we intend to pass partner's next bid unless it is another Force and would drop the bidding if he should bid either two notrump or rebid his own suit to three. If partner's response is two clubs, our first thought might be to bid two notrump but this thought should be quickly suppressed, since *the rebid to two notrump always indicates substantial additional values.* Instead, we merely bid two diamonds, intending to pass unless partner forces, since we have no support for partner's suit and our own suit is so weak.

♠ A K 10 9 6 5   ♡ A Q 6   ◊ 3 2   ♣ 3 2

High card value 9.

Since we have bid a spade, partner cannot respond with a
One-Over-One. If he responds with two hearts we bid three
hearts, while if his response is two clubs or two diamonds
we bid two spades. If over our second-round two-spade
bid he bids two notrump, we bid three notrump. If he bids
three spades we bid four, while if he merely rebids his own
suit we are compelled to pass.

♠ A J 8 7 2   ♡ A K 2   ◊ 6 5 4   ♣ 7 3

High card value 8½.

Again if partner bids two hearts over our one spade, we
raise to three, while over a two-diamond or two-club response we merely bid two spades. If over our second-round
two-spade bid partner bids two notrump, we bid three notrump. If he bids three spades we bid four. If he rebids his
own suit we pass. So far this development of the bidding
is identical with that of the very much stronger preceding
hand. A difference will occur in the event that partner
first responds with two diamonds and then over two spades
bids three clubs. With the preceding hand we could afford
to bid three notrump, but with this hand we can only return to three diamonds.

♠ 6 2   ♡ A K 6 4 3 2   ◊ A 2   ♣ 5 4 3

High card value 8.

If partner responds with one spade our rebid is two hearts.
If he bids two spades we pass, while if he bids two notrump
we bid three. If his second bid is three diamonds or three
clubs we merely bid three hearts, a Sign-off. If partner's

response is two diamonds or two clubs we also bid two hearts, intending to bid three notrump if he bids two; to pass if he rebids his own suit, and to bid three hearts if he bids a new suit. Following any Exploratory response and our subsequent rebid, if partner raises our hearts to three we bid four.

♠ AKxxx   ♡ Axx   ◇ Kxx   ♣ xx

High card value 10.

Over a two-heart response to our one-spade bid we bid three hearts and if partner now bids three spades we bid four spades, while if he bids three notrump or four hearts we pass. Similarly, we bid three diamonds over a two-diamond response, intending to contract for five diamonds if partner bids four. Over two clubs it is best to bid two spades.

♠ A   ♡ KQJxxx   ◇ Axx   ♣ Kxx

High card value 11½.

Over any Exploratory Response we bid three hearts, a Qualified Game Force.

♠ AQ10xxx   ♡ Axxx   ◇ xx   ♣ x

High card value 7.

Over two hearts we bid three hearts. Over two diamonds or two clubs we bid two spades, intending to pass a rebid of partner's suit. Should partner's second bid be two notrump or three of the other minor suit, we sign off with three spades. If, however, on his second bid, he raises our spades to three, we bid four.

♠ Ax   ♡ Ax   ◇ K10xxxx   ♣ Kxx

High card value 10.

Over a response of one spade or one heart we bid two diamonds. If partner now rebids his suit or bids the other major, we bid two notrump, inviting game. If his second bid is three diamonds or two notrump we bid three no-trump. If partner's response is two clubs, we raise to three clubs.

♠ A x   ♡ A Q x x x   ◇ A Q x   ♣ x x x

High card value 11.

If partner responds with one spade our best second bid is probably one notrump, a slight underbid, made with the definite intention of continuing if partner can find a further bid.* If partner's response is two clubs our second bid is two notrump, while if he bids two diamonds we should raise to three diamonds.

DEVELOPMENT OF THE BIDDING WITH MULTIPLE SUIT HANDS

The following two- and three-suit hands have been discussed briefly under the Opening bid. Let us consider them further:

♠ A K x x   ♡ Q J 10 x x x   ◇ A x   ♣ x

High card value 9½.

Bid one heart. This hand, which is very powerful distribu-tionally, should be bid as a one-suiter. If partner responds with two hearts, we can afford to jump immediately to four, while if he bids one notrump we can bid three hearts, intending to play the hand at game in that suit. Similarly, over partner's Exploratory bid of either two diamonds or two clubs, we bid three hearts. Should his initial re-

---

* Unless partners can find a second bid over this one notrump, the chance of missing a game is slight indeed.

sponse be one spade, we would recognize the fit and offer a strong Slam try by bidding four spades. This four-spade bid introduces an interesting principle which is illustrated as follows:

	Bidder	Responder
(a)	1 ♠	3 ♠ (A Forcing response)
(b)	1 ♠	4 ♠ (A Jump to game)

Each shows approximately the same playing strength, but

	Bidder	Responder
(c)	1 ♡	1 ♠
	3 ♠	

is a Qualified Game Force, since the Responding Hand might be justified in passing.

	Bidder	Responder
(d)	1 ♡	1 ♠
	4 ♠	

is a definite Slam Invitation, which says: "Partner, my hand is so strong that I will not take even the slight risk that you may pass a three-spade bid."

♠ K J x x x   ♡ A x   ◇ A K x x x   ♣ x

High card value 10½.

Opening bid one spade. This hand is particularly strong if partner's hand fits either spades or diamonds. After a two-spade response we must not only be sure of reaching game, but should mildly invite a Slam. A one-notrump response will warrant our making a Game-Forcing bid of three diamonds on the second round. A Jump response in our suit or in notrump will indicate a Slam. In the Exploratory response, however, lurks the danger of a misfit and consequently after such a response we must proceed cautiously. After a two-heart response, we can afford to make the strong Skip Level Shift to three diamonds, since if partner now bids three hearts we can bid four hearts. Over a two-club bid we bid two diamonds only, and if partner then bids three clubs, we should pass.

♠ K Q J x   ♡ A K x x x   ◇ Q x   ♣ x x

High card value 9½.

Bid one spade. Should partner respond with two spades we could afford to make a Temporary Forcing bid of three hearts, hoping that he could then bid four spades, for we should have to pass three spades. In case his initial response is one notrump we bid two hearts, intending to pass if he replies with two spades, or two notrump. If he raises our two hearts to three we bid four hearts. If partner's response is a Jump to three spades we should bid four spades, *not four hearts,* since that bid would be a Slam invitation. Should partner respond with two notrump we bid three hearts; if he responds with four spades we pass. Should his response be three notrump we bid four hearts, a mild Slam invitation. With this hand the Exploratory responses present no problem. Over two diamonds or two clubs, two hearts is the obvious reply. If partner bids three hearts we bid four. If he bids two notrump we bid three notrump. If he returns to two spades or rebids his own suit to three, we pass. If partner bids three of the other minor suit, we bid three notrump.

♠ K Q J x   ♡ K Q J x x   ◇ A x   ♣ K x

High card value 12.

Opening bid one heart. With this very fine hand, we contract for game if partner offers the slightest encouragement. If partner's response is one notrump we bid two spades (a strong Skip Level Shift), intending to bid three notrump over two notrump, or four hearts over three hearts. Over an Exploratory response of two diamonds or two clubs we also make the strong bid of two spades.

♠ x x   ♡ A K x x   ◇ A Q x x   ♣ J x x

High card value 9½.

Bid one heart. While this hand has two biddable suits, nevertheless, because of its balanced distribution a response of one notrump or two hearts should be passed, and one notrump should be bid over one spade. If partner makes the Exploratory response of two clubs, we are forced to the Level Shift of two diamonds. We now intend to pass a second response of two hearts, three clubs or three diamonds; to bid two notrump over two spades; or three notrump over two notrump.

♠ A K x x   ♡ x x   ◇ x x x   ♣ A K x x

High card value 10.

Another balanced two-suiter. Bid one club. If partner bids one notrump or two clubs we pass. If he bids one heart or one diamond we make the Level Shift bid of one spade, intending to pass any non-forcing rebid by partner.

♠ A K x x   ♡ x   ◇ A Q J x   ♣ x x x x

High card value 9½.

Opening bid one diamond. If partner bids one notrump or two diamonds we pass. If he bids two clubs we raise to three, and should he bid one heart we bid one spade, a Level Shift.

♠ A K x x   ♡ x x x   ◇ K Q x x   ♣ K 10

High card value 10.

A balanced hand. Opening bid one spade. If partner responds with two spades or one notrump, we pass. If he responds with two hearts, we are just strong enough to bid two notrump, while over two clubs, we bid two diamonds. Over a two-diamond response we bid three diamonds.

EXAMPLES OF THREE-SUITERS

The following examples are three-suiters:

♠ A K 3 2   ♡ A 9 3 2   ◇ 6   ♣ Q J 3 2

High card value 9½.

Opening bid one club. Over one spade or one heart the best bid is a Jump Raise to three in the suit. Over one diamond the best bid is the Level Shift to one spade. If partner's first response is two clubs, we bid two spades, intending to pass if he signs off with three clubs. If his first response is two notrump we bid three spades; if he then bids three notrump, we pass. We have left the one-notrump response, which is very unlikely over our one-club, to the last; if partner does make it, we pass.

♠ A K 3 2   ♡ x   ◇ K J x x   ♣ A K x x

High card value 12½.

Opening bid one diamond. With this very fine hand we intend to show all three suits if necessary. If partner bids one notrump we bid two spades, a Skip Level Shift, and if he now bids two notrump, we bid three clubs. Should partner respond with one spade, we bid four spades (a Slam try). Over one heart we bid one spade, intending if partner bids two hearts to bid two notrump. Over two clubs, we first bid three spades, a Game Force, and subsequently five clubs, strongly inviting a Slam. A simple two-diamond response would indicate a probable game in that suit. Over two notrump, we investigate Slam possibilities by bidding our other two suits.

♠ A x x x   ♡ A Q x x   ◊ A Q x x   ♣ x

High card value 11.

Opening bid one spade, a shaded biddable suit. Should partner bid one notrump we bid two hearts, and if he now bids two notrump, we bid three diamonds. Should partner raise our spades to two we bid three hearts, intending if he bids three spades to contract for a spade game. The reader will note that this hand would be particularly powerful opposite any fit. Obviously, the main consideration is to find it. Should partner respond with two hearts or two diamonds we jump to four, while over two clubs we make a Level Shift bid of two hearts.

Part II

CHAPTER XI

General Principles Applying to Defensive and Competitive Bidding

IN PART I of the book, we discussed attacking bidding, aimed at an eventual game or part-score contract. We stressed the word "safe" in connection with part scores and explained that frequently it is good tactics to gamble for a doubtful game or Slam, but that when your aim is only for a part score, you should take no risk.

In Defensive and Competitive bidding *safety* becomes much more important, since at any time you may expect a Double with a resultant penalty. Accordingly, the risk taken must be commensurate with the possible objective. This is the *Principle of Risk versus Gain*. For instance, suppose you are second hand, vulnerable, and hold

♠ A K x x x　♡ x　◇ A K x x　♣ x x

and the dealer, not vulnerable, opens with a Pre-emptive bid of four hearts. You must overcall with four spades. This action exposes you to a penalty which on some rare occasion will be severe, but the probabilities are that you will make your contract. In other words, the objective, which is a vulnerable game, is large enough and the probability of attaining the objective great enough to justify the risk. On the other hand, suppose you are not vulnerable and your opponents have reached four hearts on normal bidding. You are certain that should you bid four spades they will double and set you two tricks. While this penalty is less than the value of game, if you have reason to believe that they may not make their four-heart contract, why not pass and gamble on a possible profit, rather than accept a certain loss?

In the great bulk of defensive situations we have set a definite Limit of Risk, namely, two tricks, vulnerable, or three tricks, not vulnerable.

In subsequent chapters, we shall emphasize the danger of exposing yourself to greater penalties; nevertheless, it should be borne in mind that there are some hands with which it is folly to take even a 100-point set, and others with which you must risk as much as 1400 points.

PENALTY EQUIVALENTS

The following table will serve as a guide to the Attacking Side in determining when to double, and the Defending Side in estimating exactly what risks they are taking:

A penalty of 50 or 100 points is negligible, and less than the value of part score.

A penalty of 200 or 300 points is more than the value of part score but less than the value of game.

A penalty of 500 points is approximately equivalent to game. This penalty should not be incurred unless you are certain that the opponents' game contract cannot be defeated.

The above approximations are the result of combining our experience with accurate mathematical calculations, and are correct for all practical purposes.

CHAPTER XII

Specialized Opening Bids

In PART I we stated that the bidding may be opened for one of the following reasons:

  (A) To launch the attack.
  (B) To guard against being shut out by the adversaries.
  (C) To obtain the most favorable lead against an anticipated adverse contract.
  (D) To mislead the opponents or interrupt their normal exchange of information.

In Part I we considered only Opening bids to launch the attack and stated that to qualify as an Opening bid a hand must fulfill the following requirements.

  1. It must contain a minimum high card strength (7 to $9\frac{1}{2}$, depending upon distribution).
  2. It must have a logical rebid over any Exploratory response by partner. This logical rebid may consist of ability to repeat the initial declaration, bid a new suit, raise partner's suit, or bid notrump.

In this part of the book we shall consider the following additional Opening bids made with hands which do not satisfy the above requirements but, nevertheless, should be opened for tactical or positional reasons:

  1. The Opening bid to interrupt the adversaries' nor-

mal exchange of information. This is the Pre-emptive Opening bid of three or more in a suit.*

2. The Opening bid with a freak two-suiter. Such hands contain at least ten cards in two suits. In first or second position we may shade our high card requirements to the extent of opening with a value of 6 ½—an average hand. In third or fourth position, where we need not fear that partner will contract for a Slam, we may reduce our high card holding to as low as 5 ½, particularly when we have the major suits.

3. The Opening bid to obtain the most favorable lead against an anticipated adverse contract. This bid is made in third position only.

4. The borderline bid without a rebid. Such a bid may be made in third or fourth position with high card strength somewhere in the borderline zone (7 to 9), but with factors of distribution, etc., that do not make the hand strong enough to rebid over an Exploratory response by partner. These bids are usually made in the expectation of obtaining a partial score, and from their very nature should not be rebid unless the bidding develops in an unusually favorable manner.

THE OPENING PRE-EMPTIVE BID

The Development Principle consists of bidding toward the final contract in a slow and logical fashion rather than in a rapid hit-or-miss manner. When we make an Opening pre-emptive bid of three or four of a suit, we are obviously and intentionally discarding this Development Principle. In declining to make use of its advantages we give this clear message to partner: "My hand is such that I fear

---

* Opening three- and four-bids may also be made in fourth position as a definite attacking measure.

normal development of the bidding will permit our opponents to derive a greater advantage from the exchange of information at a low level than we will."

The Pre-emptive bid is nearly always made with a below-average hand in an effort to prevent a normal exchange of information by the opponents. It is primarily defensive, but on the other hand, there are always offensive possibilities. When pre-empting you should be sure that your suit has great strength and enough solidity to require no support from partner. In other words, the playing trick * strength of the various bids in accordance with the Limit of Risk should be as follows:

The three-bid not vulnerable...6 to 7 playing-tricks
The four-bid not vulnerable ...7 to 9 playing-tricks
The three-bid vulnerable......7 to 8 playing-tricks
The four-bid vulnerable ......8 to 9 playing-tricks

Note that the highest limit of playing-tricks for a Pre-emptive bid is nine. The reason for this is that if our hand includes more than nine playing-tricks we must always contemplate Slam possibilities and therefore should permit the bidding to develop normally. It will also be noted that we do not consider the Pre-emptive bid of five. Obviously, there is no point in opening the bidding with five of a major suit. With a hand containing eight or nine playing-tricks, such a bid would jeopardize game, while four would probably be sufficient to shut out the opponents. A Pre-emptive bid of five of a minor suit is unsound. To make the bid, at least eight playing-tricks would be required and such a hand might well play at three notrump.

When a Pre-emptive bid is made in first or second position it should definitely deny the holding of more than

* Playing tricks are the tricks you expect to take as declarer.

average high card strength (6½), since otherwise we should bid one and permit the bidding to develop logically. In third position, after partner has passed, we may, at times, inject a Pre-emptive bid with a hand that has a fairly strong high card value, provided that our high card holding does not indicate Slam possibilities. In fourth position, Opening three or four bids must be given very special consideration. In that position the question of defending is eliminated, as we can pass if we feel that our hand is purely defensive. The fact that neither opponent cared to open the bidding makes it unlikely that either will be able to overcall an opening three- or four-bid. Accordingly, if we see a good chance to make a score it may be worth while to pre-empt. Furthermore, in fourth position, we may depend on our partner for some of the missing strength; otherwise one of the opponents would have been able to bid. Therefore, if we make a Pre-emptive *game bid* in this position, partner must never invite a Slam, while a Pre-emptive bid of less than game should only be raised with a substantial holding.

EXAMPLES OF PRE-EMPTIVE HANDS

Examples of hands in the Pre-emptive class are as follows:

♠ K J 10 9 5 3 2   ♡ x x   ◇ x x   ♣ x x
High card value 2½.

This should be passed. It is not strong enough for a Pre-emptive bid.

♠ K J 10 9 5 3 2   ♡ x x x x   ◇ x   ♣ x
High card value 2½.

This is the same as the previous hand except that we

have changed the distribution of the side suits. Such a freak holding indicates additional playing strength, and we can afford to bid three spades if not vulnerable.

♠ x x   ♡ K Q J x x x x   ◇ x x   ♣ x x

High card value 3½.

This hand should take six tricks and hence warrants a non-vulnerable bid of three hearts.

♠ x   ♡ x x   ◇ A K Q J x x x   ♣ x x x

High card value 6½.

This hand presents several distinct possibilities. Although it has a high card value of but 6½, it has seven sure playing-tricks. Therefore, if we pre-empt in first or second position we must realize that there are distinct chances of missing a game in notrump. In third position, although there is a chance that our partner's holding may be such that three notrump can be made, there is a stronger possibility that the opponents can make four hearts or four spades. Therefore, it is advisable to pre-empt as strongly as possible. Not vulnerable, this would indicate a four-diamond bid; vulnerable, a three-diamond bid. In fourth position the situation is different. The fact that no other player has bid indicates that we should make an effort to score, particularly as we know that partner must hold some of the missing high cards. We should bid three diamonds, hoping that partner is strong enough to bid three notrump.

♠ K Q J x x x x   ♡ A x x x   ◇ —   ♣ x

High card value 6½.

In first or second position this hand shows some Slam

possibilities, and we should not make a Pre-emptive bid. Probably our best tactics are to bid one spade originally and subsequently to be guided by the normal development of the bidding. The reader should remember that Pre-emptive bids are not designed for the purpose of reaching Slam contracts, and that such bids always ask partner not to try for a Slam unless his holding is tremendous. In third or fourth position we pre-empt with four spades, since it is more important to shut out the opponents than to investigate the slight Slam possibilities.

♠ A K Q J x x x   ♡ A x   ◇ x x   ♣ x x

High card value 9½.

This hand with a high card value of 9½ obviously meets all the requirements for a one-spade bid, and that bid should be made in first or second position. After partner passes, there would be no likely Slam possibility, and we bid four spades.

♠ A K Q J x x   ♡ K Q J x   ◇ K x x   ♣ —

High card value 12.

This hand should be bid as one spade in any position. Even though partner has passed, we still see distinct Slam possibilities. Furthermore, the possibility that the opponents will profit from the ability to exchange information is negligible when compared with the advantages that we may derive. This example is given as a type of hand which should *never* be bid pre-emptively.

THE OPENING BID WITH A FREAK TWO-SUITER

Experience has shown that any hand with ten or more cards, distributed in two suits, has a tremendous offensive value if partner can fit either of them. Furthermore, if the holding is of that nature, there is great likelihood of there being other freak distributions. Consequently, if such a hand is passed originally its holder might find it impossible ever to bid except at great danger of a heavy penalty.

If in addition to this freak distribution, a player is also blessed with a substantial high card holding, he would naturally open the bidding in a straight attacking manner, while with no high cards at all, he must pass. In case his high card holding is average or slightly below ($5\frac{1}{2}$ to $6\frac{1}{2}$), he must carefully consider the advisability of opening the bidding on his shaded high card value. The considerations are:

1. *Position at the Table.* In first or second position, a substantial shading may misinform partner and result in his arriving at an unmakable Slam contract. However, with an average hand ($6\frac{1}{2}$), we are but half a point below the requirements for a normal bid and our distribution should compensate. In third or fourth position, we have no fear of arriving at a Slam and so may shade to $5\frac{1}{2}$.

2. *Game Possibilities.* If we hold both major suits and partner can raise either of them, in spite of the fact that our combined high card holding may be less than half the pack, we should have a good play for game.

3. *Vulnerability.* Any irregular action is fraught with some danger. Hence we must be particularly careful when vulnerable.

The following are examples of such bids:

♠ A x x x x x　♡ K J x x x　◇ x　♣ x

High card value $5\frac{1}{2}$.

Bid one spade in third or fourth position.

♠ x   ♡ xx   ◇ K Q J xx   ♣ K xxxx

High card value 5½.

Bid one diamond in third position only as a strictly defensive and lead-directing measure.

♠ K 10 xxx   ♡ Q x   ◇ A J xxx   ♣ x

High card value 6½.

This hand is too weak offensively to warrant opening the bidding in first or second position, since we have no means of sustaining the attack should partner bid two hearts. In third or fourth position, we bid one spade, intending to bid two diamonds over a two-club response, and to pass a bid of two hearts or two spades.

♠ x   ♡ —   ◇ A J xxxx   ♣ A 10 xxxx

High card value 6½.

Bid a diamond in any position. This hand is so strong distributionally that we are willing to *attack* in the minor suits with a shaded high card holding.

THE THIRD HAND DEFENSIVE OR LEAD-DIRECTING BID

We restrict this bid to third position since it is extremely inadvisable to make it either in first or second, and it is totally unnecessary in fourth position. However, if Third Hand is below average, its holder is in the unique position of knowing that as neither First nor second Hand could open the bidding it is more than likely that Fourth Hand can and will open. Moreover, he is quite certain that the opponents will fulfill a game or part-score contract. Suppose Third Hand holds

♠ K x x   ♡ Q x x x   ◇ K J x   ♣ Q x x

High card value 6½.

His mental observations are: "There is little I can do about this. If Fourth Hand becomes declarer, as is probable, my partner must lead. Whatever suit he leads will find a supporting honor in my hand. If I bid we will probably get into trouble. Therefore, I pass."

Suppose, however, the Third Hand holds

♠ x x   ♡ x x   ◇ x x x   ♣ A K x x x x

High card value 5.

He reasons: "Fourth Hand will almost surely open the bidding and his partner will respond. If I bid my clubs at the necessary level (two or three), I may be doubled and severely penalized; if I fail to bid my clubs and Fourth Hand becomes declarer, my partner will not know what to lead. Therefore, it behooves me to anticipate this eventuality by bidding a club." This reasoning is the fundamental basis for the third-hand, Lead-Directing bid.

A second advantage of the Lead-Directing bid is that our opponents cannot be sure whether we have a real Opening bid or just a lead-director. For this reason they are likely to stop short of a game bid which they could make.

The use of Lead-Directing bids involves some danger, since we run the following risks:

1. That our partner will blindly continue the bidding to a point where we will incur a serious penalty.

2. That our partner will double the opponents at a contract which they can make.

On the other hand, partner should allow for the fact that our Third-Hand bid may be shaded, especially if we pass thereafter; therefore, if the opponents subsequently secure the contract, partner should double on the strength of his own hand, not on ours.

The matter of vulnerability is of particular importance in making Lead-Directing bids. When not vulnerable, little risk would be run with a hand such as the following:

♠ x x   ♡ x x   ◇ K x x   ♣ K Q x x x x

High card value 5.

When vulnerable, however, a club bid on this hand might result in a two- or three-trick set and therefore should be eschewed.

THE BORDERLINE BID WITHOUT A REBID

Made Only in Third or Fourth Position

As previously stated the object of Contract Bridge is to win as many points as possible with good cards and to lose the minimum with bad cards. In third or fourth position, if we believe that our hand is the best at the table, we must consider an Opening bid. With such a hand there is a far better chance of our side scoring than the opponents. For example, consider the following hands:

♠ A K x x   ♡ A J x   ◇ x x x   ♣ x x x

High card value 8½.

While this hand has no rebid, nevertheless, we are certainly more than willing to play for eight tricks in whatever suit partner might choose as a response to a one-spade bid.

The reason that we do not open the bidding in first or second position on hands such as the above lies in the Principle of Anticipation. If we open the bidding and our partner responds with two clubs, two diamonds, or two hearts, we find ourselves in the embarrassing predicament of not knowing what to do. If we rebid, we may get too high and be penalized severely; while if we pass and it turns out that partner had a strong hand, we will have missed a game.

In third or fourth position, we do not expect to make game, since partner's pass has limited the strength of his hand. To make game, he needs either an Opening bid (which his pass has denied) or a terrific freak that fits with our hand. Therefore, we open, intending to pass practically any response by partner.

It will be noted that the above example hand is almost strong enough for a normal Opening bid. This is emphasized because we do not wish to imply that we make a regular habit of opening the bidding in third or fourth position without a rebid. Even a hand as strong as

$$\spadesuit \ A\,x\,x\,x \qquad \heartsuit \ A\,x\,x \qquad \diamondsuit \ x\,x\,x \qquad \clubsuit \ K\,x\,x$$

High card value 8.

should be passed in any position; while weaker hands such as

$$\spadesuit \ A\,x \qquad \heartsuit \ K\,x\,x \qquad \diamondsuit \ K\,x\,x\,x\,x \qquad \clubsuit \ x\,x\,x$$

High card value 7.

are not worth considering.

CHAPTER XIII

Competitive Bidding

So FAR we have considered only those bidding situations in which the opponents remain quiescent; and, just as it is easy to hit a tennis ball in proper form when your instructor strokes it softly to a convenient spot, so it is comparatively simple to bid properly when there is no interference. In actual play your opponents frequently enter the bidding, sometimes solely for the purpose of embarrassing you; at other times they do so with good hands. Unless you are equipped to handle these situations, you will find yourself playing hands in unsatisfactory contracts.

The most important rule in such instances is *believe your partner,* except in those rare cases when strong bidding by conservative opponents indicates that he may not have his full values.

To simplify discussion, we make use of the following definitions and diagram:

> *Attacking Side*—The Opening Bidder and his partner.
>
> *Defending Side*—The opponents, even though these positions may sometimes become reversed.
>
> *Bidder*—The player who opens the bidding.
>
> *Responder*—The partner of the Bidder.

Senior—The opponent to the left of the Bidder.
Junior—The opponent to the right of the Bidder.

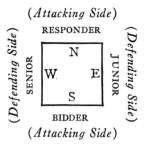

(*Attacking Side*)

ACTION BY SENIOR AFTER AN OPENING BID OF ONE
OF A SUIT

1. *The Pass* with a hand not strong enough to risk an overcall.

2. *The Pass with Defense, sometimes called the Trap Pass,* with certain strong hands which will produce practically as many tricks on defense as on attack.

3. *Simple Suit Overcalls.* Such overcalls should be made to indicate:

    (a) The possibility of fulfilling a contract ourselves.

    (b) The proper line of defense against a final declaration by the Attacking Side.

    (c) The possibility of continuing the bidding and sacrificing, rather than letting the opponents secure game or Slam.

In discussing the Opening bid, we first stressed high card requirements, and then, in the case of borderline hands (7 to 9) proceeded to consider playing strength as the determining factor. In overcalling, however, our playing strength becomes by far the more important consideration. It is rare indeed that we can afford to take any action which will risk a set of over three tricks, not vulnerable, or two tricks, vulnerable.

Our experience has shown that the habit of making overcalls without sufficient playing strength is about as expensive as any a Bridge player can acquire. *Responder* has the immediate opportunity of doubling, and Senior is crushed between the upper and nether millstones.

Of course some high card strength is essential for an overcall since otherwise to bid would be merely pointless. In general, we recommend a high card value of at least 5, though it may in rare instances be shaded if the suit is long and the high cards are concentrated in that suit.

EXAMPLES OF OVERCALLS

Examples of an overcall of a one-heart bid are as follows:

♠ K Q 10 9 x x   ♡ x   ◇ x x x   ♣ x x x

High card value 3.

Not vulnerable bid one spade. Should Junior raise our bid, we can probably defend at four spades against a contemplated four-heart bid by the Attacking Side. At the same time we have told Junior what to lead in case Responder becomes the declarer. Vulnerable, we cannot afford to overcall, since the probability of a three-trick set is too great. Furthermore, reversing our spades and diamonds we could not afford to overcall if not vulnerable, since a bid of two diamonds would risk a four-trick set.

♠ A K x x x   ♡ x x x   ◇ A x   ♣ K x x

High card value 10.

This is a very strong hand and suggests distinct game

possibilities if partner can support our spades. On the other hand, unless partner can take some voluntary action we see there is no chance of game, and merely bid one spade whether vulnerable or not.

♠ AKQ9 ♡ xx ◇ Axxx ♣ xxx

High card value 9.

We have a sound one-spade overcall, vulnerable or not.

When opening the bidding, we have stressed willingness to bid very weak four-card suits, and have shaded our requirements even more when responding to an Opening bid. However, in overcalling, with the risk of an immediate Double, we lean the other way. Even to overcall at the range of one, a strong four-card suit is necessary. When a bid in the range of two is contemplated, we are even careful with a five- or six-card suit, and pay particular attention to the solidity of the suit. For instance, K J 10 9 6 4 is safer than A Q 7 6 4 3.

♠ Ax ♡ xxx ◇ AQxxx ♣ Kxx

High card value 9.

The size of the small diamonds is the determining factor in whether or not this hand is a proper two-diamond over-call. Should the three small diamonds be the 4 3 2, it is not a proper overcall; while should they be the 9 8 7, we would have an overcall but only if not vulnerable.

♠ xx ♡ xxx ◇ KQJ10xx ♣ xx

High card value 3½.

Not vulnerable, bid two diamonds. Vulnerable, you should pass.

4. *The Jump Suit Overcall.* This bid is one of the spe-

cialized features of the Four Aces System and has been developed to the point where it is one of our strongest defensive weapons. *It is made purely on playing strength and conveys the definite information that the hand is weak in high cards.*

Its primary purpose is to prevent the opponents from exchanging information at a low level, and hence to make their subsequent bidding difficult. Its secondary purpose is to inform our partner that he must rely solely upon his own cards for tricks against an adverse declaration.

The Jump Suit Overcall is very similar to the Opening Pre-emptive bid and should be bid to its own limit at once; i.e., to the point where you may expect to be set not more than three tricks, not vulnerable, or two tricks, vulnerable. Remember, the higher the Jump, the harder it is for Responder to know what to do.

Examples of Jump Suit Overcalls over an Opening one-heart bid are:

♠ K Q J x x x   ♡ x x   ◊ Q J x x   ♣ x

Not vulnerable, we recommend a bid of three spades. This hand satisfies the requirements for a Jump Overcall, and this bid may make it difficult for adversaries to reach the best contract.

♠ x x   ♡ x   ◊ x x   ♣ Q J 10 9 x x x x

This hand is entirely defenseless. We feel certain when the Opening one-heart bid is made that the Attacking Side will reach game or Slam. If vulnerable, we might as well grin and bear it, but if not vulnerable, we bid four clubs, risking a maximum penalty of 700 points. With this hand we exceed our normal Limit of Risk because we greatly fear a Slam. A bid of three clubs is not sufficiently preemptive to disturb the opponents.

♠ K Q J x x x x   ♡ A x   ♢ x x   ♣ x x

Although this hand is average in high cards, it probably holds but one defensive trick against any adverse suit declaration, and unless partner has defense, the opponents have a probable game. Accordingly, we make the immediate Jump Overcall of three spades, vulnerable, or four spades, not vulnerable. In the event that Responder bids four hearts over our vulnerable three-spade bid, Junior should raise us to four spades with a hand such as the following:

♠ A x   ♡ x x x   ♢ A x x x   ♣ x x x x

Had we merely overcalled with one spade, and Responder then bid three hearts, Junior would have been forced to pass.

5. *Attacking Overcalls by Senior.* If Senior has a hand that warrants an immediate attack against the Opening bid, he has three courses of action: the Takeout Double, the Notrump Overcall, and the Overcall in Opponents' Suit. The most common of these three bids is the Takeout (Informatory) Double.

This Takeout Double convention first appeared in the game of Auction Bridge about fifteen years ago, and is an absolutely necessary feature of Contract. If Senior, over an Opening bid of one of a suit, doubles, he implies: "Partner, I want you to bid. My hand is so strong that in spite of our opponents having opened the bidding, I still see distinct possibilities of game. However, should you hold a hand with great strength in the opponents' suit you may pass this Double, whereupon we can probably inflict a substantial penalty."

The Overcall in the Opponents' Bid Suit approximates the Opening two-bid in general strength, and is forcing to game. This bid is the strongest action Senior can take. The distribution is of such a nature that Senior does not care to risk the possibility of Junior passing a Takeout Double.*

Frequently, we will have a hand in which a substantial part of our strength is located in the suit bid by our opponent, and if we double we will not be strong enough to make a second-round bid of two notrump. With such a hand, we make a strength overcall of one notrump to avoid future guesses.

Examples of Attacking Overcalls are as follows:

♠ A Q x x   ♡ x   ◇ A Q x x   ♣ A K x x

High card value 13.

Over a bid of one heart, Senior makes a Takeout Double, being prepared to raise any suit bid by partner. Over a bid of one diamond or one club he also makes a Takeout Double, being prepared to bid a spade if partner bids a heart. Over a bid of one spade, on the other hand, he cannot afford to make a Takeout Double since he has no preparation for the expected response by partner of two hearts. Therefore, he makes a trap pass and waits in ambush.

♠ A Q 10 9 x   ♡ A Q J x x   ◇ K Q J   ♣ —

High card value 12.

Over one club, holding the above hand we bid two clubs, absolutely forcing our partner to bid. If he has as many as three of either major suit, we should make game, while we do not want our partner to pass a Double of one club.

---

* If Responder passes, Junior is forced to bid. If Junior holds any suit of four cards or more, other than the one bid by the opponents, he should respond in that suit. Otherwise, he should bid two notrump.

Over a one-diamond bid, we double, since we can afford to have it left in, and also since we are prepared to bid both our suits in the event that Junior responds with two clubs. In case the Opening bid has been either a heart or a spade we also double, intending to bid the other major at a later stage.

♠ Q 10 6 4   ♡ Q 10 6 4   ◇ A Q   ♣ A K x

High card value 11.

Over an Opening bid of one club or one diamond, we double, as we are prepared for a bid of either major suit by partner. Over a spade or a heart by a vulnerable opponent, we recommend a trap pass; by a non-vulnerable opponent, a notrump overcall.

♠ x   ♡ x   ◇ A K x x x x   ♣ A K x x x

High card value 10.

Over a bid of one spade or one heart we bid two diamonds. In spite of the great strength of this hand we do not double because such a double is almost certain to provoke a response by Junior in the other major suit, which response will not help our bidding problem. Furthermore, should Responder jump to four of the original suit we would have no chance to show both our diamonds and clubs and would not know what action to take. On the other hand, a two-diamond bid is perfectly safe. It is very unlikely that three passes will follow this bid, and we can afford to show our clubs as high as five on the second round. This hand is very important as it illustrates the general principle of *not doubling with two-suited hands*. The ideal Double has either preparation for three suits or great strength in one suit.

♠ A K Q x x x   ♡ A x   ◇ K x x   ♣ x x

High card value 11.

Double an Opening bid of one heart, one diamond, or one club. With this very strong hand, irrespective of partner's response, we can afford to show the spades. In the previous illustrations our Doubles were made with hands which indicated the necessity of finding the best suit. With this hand we intend to play either spades or notrump unless partner has a most unusual distribution. By first doubling and then bidding spades, we inform partner of our strength.

♠ A x   ♡ x x   ◇ A K Q x x x   ♣ A x x

High card value 12.

Over an Opening bid of one spade or one club we prefer the unusual bid of two notrump to a Double. Although we desire our partner to bid for game with very little strength, we can probably make game only in notrump. Over an Opening bid of one heart, however, we should not make the two-notrump bid, for the obvious reason that we hold no stopper in hearts. Accordingly, we are forced to double, and then to bid and rebid diamonds in the event that partner responds in spades or clubs.

♠ x x x   ♡ x x   ◇ A K 4 3 2   ♣ A Q 2

High card value 9.

With this hand a Takeout Double would be both pointless and foolish. It is not even worth an overcall at the range of two, but you may bid one diamond over one club.

Retaining the same high cards but changing the distribution, viz.

♠ x x x x   ♡ x   ◇ A K x x   ♣ A Q x x

you have a sound Double of a one-heart bid. Here you are prepared for any suit partner bids. In order to double without great high card strength, you should have very fine distribution.

SUMMARY OF SENIOR'S ACTION AFTER AN OPENING BID OF ONE IN A SUIT

The principal point for Senior to bear in mind in determining whether or not to overcall is playing strength, and while a hand with a high card value as low as 3 may warrant an overcall, hands with as much as 11 may properly be passed. Similarly, the Takeout Double is primarily distributional, but in addition it should have a high card strength of 9½.

As a guide in overcalling, we suggest the following rules:

1. The Jump Suit Overcall may be made almost wholly irrespective of high card strength and purely on playing tricks.

2. Other overcalls, in general, should have a value of 5 or more, but occasionally may be made with as little as 3, not vulnerable.

3. The Takeout Double is an attacking measure, and although primarily distributional must indicate substantial high card values. To make this Double, the high card holding should be equivalent to that of a very good Opening bid. Accordingly, we suggest 9½ as the normal high card strength for this Double, though on occasion it may be shaded to as low as 8, for example:

♠ K Q 10 x   ♡ K Q J x   ◊ Q J 10 x   ♣ x

High card value 8.

This hand, owing to its fine distribution, is strong enough to double an Opening one-club bid.

4. A Notrump Overcall should be fully as strong in high cards as an original one notrump, but may occasionally be made with one suit—other than that bid by the opponents—unstopped.

5. The Overcall in the Opponents' Suit is forcing to game, and shows a hand practically equal to an Opening two-bid.

CHAPTER XIV

Action by Responder When Senior Has Overcalled

LET us first consider the modifications of Responder's action due to an overcall by Senior.

The Opening bid of one of a suit covers a very wide range of hands. It follows that when Senior passes, the Responder is urged to make a bid, if only for the purpose of giving the Bidder a second chance in the event that his hand is close to the upper limit of strength. There is no need for Responder to bid when Senior's overcall automatically provides Bidder with the opportunity to take further action. Therefore, our first rule for Responder is: *Any Free bid by Responder must be constructive and indicate certain definite values above those necessary for a mere Chance-giving bid.*

With a hand worth two bids, we have recommended the Exploratory and Temporary-Forcing bid of a new suit. Frequently, an overcall by Senior makes it impossible for Responder to make his normal Exploratory response, and he is now compelled to bid one notrump or raise his partner's suit to two, even though his hand may be stronger than the bid indicates. Therefore, since a Free bid of one notrump or a Free Single Raise of partner's suit may be made with a hand almost strong enough for a Game

Force, and because it is not made as a mere Chance-giving bid, it must suggest game possibilities to the Bidder.

The following examples show how an overcall modifies Responder's action:

♠ K Q x x   ♡ A x x   ♢ Q J x   ♣ x x x

Opening bid one heart. Should Senior pass, we bid one spade, intending to make a second bid after partner's response to our Temporary Force. Should Senior overcall with two clubs, the hand is certainly not strong enough to bid two spades, a Temporary Force at a higher level, and therefore two hearts is the only available bid.

♠ A K x   ♡ x x x   ♢ x x x   ♣ x x x x

Opening bid one diamond, Senior passes, we bid one no-trump. However, one diamond, Senior one spade, we pass. Although we have the two top spades, we have no other possible playing tricks and must wait for partner to rebid before taking any action whatsoever.

♠ x x x   ♡ Q x x x   ♢ K x x x   ♣ J x

Opening bid one heart. If Senior passes we bid two hearts. Should Senior overcall, we would be forced to pass.

♠ K 10 x x x   ♡ A x   ♢ x x x   ♣ x x x

Opening bid one heart. We bid one spade with no intervening bid. However, should Senior bid either two clubs or two diamonds, we could not afford to make the Free bid of two spades, and should pass.

♠ x x x   ♡ A Q x x   ♢ K 10 x   ♣ A x x

High card value 9.

This hand was previously given as an example of a two-notrump bid over partner's Opening bid of one spade. However, should Senior overcall with two diamonds or two clubs, with but one stopper in opponents' suit, we prefer to make the Exploratory bid of two hearts intending to show our stopper in opponents' suit by our next bid. Should partner open with a diamond or club and Senior overcall with a spade, our best bid unquestionably would be two hearts; it is reasonable to assume that our partner having a spade stopper would then bid two notrump, whereupon we would raise to three. Should partner's second bid be three clubs or three diamonds, we would raise him to four.

♠ — ♡ K J x ◊ A Q 10 9 x x ♣ A x x x

High card value 9½.

Partner opens the bidding with one spade. In the rare event that Senior overcalls, we either double or make a Free bid of diamonds, depending on vulnerability and whether Senior is a rash or conservative player.

♠ Q J x x ♡ x ◊ A x x x ♣ K x x x

High card value 6½.

Over partner's Opening one-spade bid this hand should be bid three spades, whether or not Senior overcalls.

♠ K Q x x ♡ A x ◊ x x ♣ K J 10 x x

High card value 8½.

Partner bids one club. If Senior overcalls with one diamond or one heart, our response is one spade, an Exploratory bid.

♠ K J x x ♡ J x ◊ A Q x x ♣ 10 x x

High card value 7.

Partner opens the bidding with one spade. Should Senior pass we bid two diamonds, as our hand is not quite strong enough for a jump to three spades. In the event that Senior overcalls with two hearts, we do not bid three diamonds, but bid two spades, a Free Raise.

♠ J x x x x   ♡ Q x   ◇ K J   ♣ K x x x

High card value 6.

Partner bids one heart and Senior two clubs. While most players would be strongly tempted to take action with this hand, we advise a pass. Trouble would be likely to follow any other step if the suggested Free bid of two spades were made. Responder would have no idea what to do over a second bid of either three spades or three hearts by the original Bidder. Therefore we would pass on the first round hoping that our partner would rebid.

> NOTE: *Extreme care should be exercised by Responder in making a* Free *bid either at two of a suit higher in rank than the suit bid by partner, or at three of a lower ranking suit. It is a Temporary Force on Bidder and promises still another bid by Responder. To illustrate, should the bidding go: (Bidder) one heart, (Senior) two clubs, (Responder) two spades, the original Bidder may be forced to rebid to three hearts—within one trick of game—at which point Responder should not pass.*

SUMMARY

The minimum strength for a Free bid by Responder must be substantially more than for a mere Chance bid. While it is impossible to give an exact rule for this difference, a rough-and-ready approximation may be obtained by considering that at least a King additional is required for a Free bid.

When an overcall by Senior makes it impossible for Responder to make a desired Exploratory bid, a Free bid of one notrump may be almost of two-notrump strength, and a Free Raise of partner's suit almost strong enough for a double Raise.

Finally, it is important to remember that the Free bid in a new suit by Responder is a Temporary Force.

BUSINESS (PENALTY) DOUBLES BY RESPONDER

As it is impossible to change human nature there will always be a large number of Bridge players who feel that it is their duty to bid whenever it is their turn. Such players cannot pass if their high-card holding is more than one quarter of the pack; for this reason such atrocities as the following are committed:

Opening bid one spade, and Senior bids two diamonds holding

♠ x x x   ♡ x x x   ◇ A K x x   ♣ A x x

Opening bid one diamond, and Senior bids one heart holding

♠ x x   ♡ A K x x   ◇ Q J x x   ♣ x x x

Against players who are prone to make such overcalls, or even against slightly more conservative players who wait for a hand such as the following to overcall with two diamonds

♠ x x   ♡ A x x   ◇ A Q 5 3 2   ♣ K x x

you will find frequent opportunities for the use of the Business Double. Furthermore, even though you anticipate no more than a two-trick set, not vulnerable, a Double is the best procedure when you do not expect to make game.

Should your partner open with one diamond, Senior bid one spade, and you hold

♠ A Q 10 8   ♡ Q J x   ♢ K x   ♣ A J x x

you may simply close your eyes and strike. While the opportunity for such rock-crusher Doubles, even against poor opponents does not come often, there are frequent opportunities for you to score more points by doubling your opponents than by playing the hand yourself.

Considerations involving a Double by the Responder of Senior's overcall are:

(1) The expectation of being able to defeat the contract.

(2) The further expectation that the amount of the penalty will be greater than your side can score as declarer, including the value of a possible game or partial score.

(3) The possibility of taking tricks against an escape bid by Junior which may in turn be doubled by your partner.

(4) Finally, in order to be able to double to the greatest advantage, partner should know that when we, as Responder, make a Business Double, he may take out holding a freak hand with either a singleton or void in the suit we double.

The following hands are examples of proper and improper Business Doubles:

♠ x   ♡ A K x x   ♢ Q 10 x x   ♣ x x x x

Opening bid, one spade, Senior two diamonds. Irrespective of vulnerability, Responder should double. He has

every right to expect to defeat the contract. There is a
possible game at notrump, but in the event that he can
take nine tricks at notrump, he will slaughter the two-
diamond contract.

♠ Q 10 x x x x   ♡ x x   ◇ x   ♣ Q J x x

Opening bid, one diamond, one spade by Senior. With this
hand Responder should pass. Even though he can defeat
one spade, he must anticipate a rescue bid. In the event
that he doubles one spade and his partner subsequently
doubles a rescue bid, disaster must overtake the partnership. If he leaves the Double in, the opponents are sure to
make their contract; if he rescues, he in turn will be
doubled.

♠ K x x   ♡ K Q 10 9   ◇ K x x   ♣ K x x

Opening bid one spade, two hearts by Senior. Responder
must realize that his side has a sure game, but that a Slam
is unlikely. As weighed against an almost certain set of
at least four tricks, the scales indicate a Double.

♠ K 10 x x   ♡ A x   ◇ Q x x   ♣ Q 9 x x

Opening bid one heart. Should Senior bid one spade, Responder's best action is merely to make a Free bid of one
notrump; while should Senior bid two clubs, he has a very
fine Double. Over a two-diamond bid a problem would be
presented which even the finest player could not solve
with any degree of certainty. The hand is not strong
enough for a bid of two spades or two notrump, while a
Raise to two hearts with but Ace-small would be decidedly
inadvisable. Finally, a Double of two diamonds might
prove to be unsatisfactory. Our recommendation is either
to double the two-diamond bid or to pass, depending upon

whether or not Senior is conservative in overcalling. Remember, even though he should make two diamonds, doubled, he would not score a game.*

* Extreme caution should be exercised in doubling contracts of two of a major suit, which, if made, will permit the opponents to score game.

CHAPTER XV

Action by Junior

IN THE event that Senior passes and Responder bids, Junior has a problem similar to that which previously faced Senior except that the bidding will probably be at a higher level. Naturally his action should be based on the same principles and considerations that guided Senior, except that they must be modified to surmount the additional difficulty of overcalling at a higher range.

Examples of action by Junior are as follows:

1. The bidding:

Bidder	Senior	Responder	Junior
1 ♠	Pass	2 ♠	?

Junior holds

♠ x   ♡ A K x x   ◇ A K x x   ♣ K Q J x

High card value 13½.

From the bidding Senior obviously has a blank hand, yet if he has five or six cards of one of Junior's three suits, a game in that suit is not unlikely. Junior therefore should double for a Takeout to determine Senior's strongest suit, being ready to raise any bid he might make and at the same time realizing that should Senior make a Business Pass a substantial set would follow.

2. The bidding:

Bidder	Senior	Responder	Junior
1 ♠	Pass	2 ♠	?

Junior holds

♠ x x   ♡ x x   ◇ x x   ♣ A Q J x x x x

High card value 4½.

This hand does not look promising, nevertheless, if not vulnerable Junior should bid three clubs, first to show Senior the correct opening lead, and second to suggest to him the possibility of defending at five clubs.

ACTION BY JUNIOR WHEN BOTH SENIOR AND RESPONDER PASS

We now come to the very rare but important situation where both Senior and Responder pass. At this point, Junior should assume that a substantial portion of the missing high cards are held by Senior and he should consider reopening the bidding, even with a weak hand. There are two dangers in reopening the bidding, namely:

(a) That the Attacking Side will successfully contract for game.

(b) That Senior will carry the bidding too high.

The first of these two dangers should be ignored, since there is no reason to assume that the opponents have misjudged the value of their combined hands to such an extent. The second danger should not be serious, if we have an intelligent partner.

We recommend that Junior reopen the bidding under the following circumstances:

(1) With a good six-card suit and a high card value of 3½ or more.

(2) With a good five-card suit and a high card value of 4½ or more.

(3) With a high card value of 6½ or more, he should either bid or double, unless his distribution is such that he believes his best chance for a profit is to set the opponents, undoubled, at their contract of one.

Examples are:

The bidding:

Bidder	Senior	Responder	Junior
1 ♠	Pass	Pass	?

Junior holds

♠ xx   ♡ xx   ◇ xxx   ♣ KQJxxx

High card value 3½.

Bid two clubs. Partner may have passed a balanced hand with spades stopped and the Ace of clubs, in which case we have a possible three notrump. In any event we can play the hand safely at three clubs.

The bidding:

Bidder	Senior	Responder	Junior
1 ♠	Pass	Pass	?

Junior holds

♠ Qxxx   ♡ Jx   ◇ Axx   ♣ Kxxx

High card value 6½.

Pass. Although partner obviously has some strength, very likely his hand is balanced, in which case it would probably be best to attempt the defeat of one spade.

The bidding:

Bidder	Senior	Responder	Junior
1 ♦	Pass	Pass	?

Junior holds

♠ A x x   ♡ K x x   ♦ x x   ♣ K x x x

High card value 7.

Double with this hand. We are prepared for any response by partner including a Business Pass.

The bidding:

Bidder	Senior	Responder	Junior
1 ♦	Pass	Pass	?

Junior holds

♠ K Q J 10 x x   ♡ A 10 x x   ♦ x   ♣ x x

Bid two spades. This bid, while not forcing, is a very strong invitation to Senior to continue as it conveys the information that Junior holds a very strong spade suit and good distribution. It should not be confused with the weak Jump Suit Overcall.

The bidding:

Bidder	Senior	Responder	Junior
1 ♦	Pass	Pass	?

Junior holds

♠ A x   ♡ A x   ♦ Q J x x x x   ♣ x x x

In this case we should pass, since it is very improbable that our side can score a game when Senior cannot afford to overcall. Furthermore, should we double, Senior will certainly be forced to take out, and no matter what he bids we are unprepared to respond. Therefore our best course is to play for the probable set of the one-diamond contract.

ACTION BY JUNIOR WHEN SENIOR OVERCALLS

This complex and important subject has been conspicuously ignored in other Bridge books.

Let us first consider the case where Responder passes Senior's overcall. In this situation Junior may pass, raise his partner's declaration, bid a new suit, or some number of notrump. Whatever action he does take, however, should be constructive, as there is no need to give Senior a *Chance* when he has merely overcalled.

This constructive action by Junior should rarely, if ever, take the form of a rescue of Senior's bid. For instance, should the bidding be one heart, one spade, pass, and Junior hold

♠ x   ♡ x x x   ◇ K Q x x x x   ♣ x x x

He should pass in preference to bidding two diamonds; although substituting the Jack-ten for two of his small diamonds, he should bid two diamonds, intending also to bid three if necessary.

The bidding:

Bidder	Senior	Responder	Junior
1 ♡	1 ♠	Pass	?

Junior holds

♠ Q x x   ♡ A x x   ◇ K x x x   ♣ Q x x

This hand offers an interesting choice of bids, but with most partners we recommend the simple Raise to two spades. Remember that when your partner opens the

bidding you must always allow for the possibility of a
weak four-card suit; when he overcalls you may nearly
always count on him for at least five.

The bidding:

Bidder	Senior	Responder	Junior
1 ♠	2 ♣	Pass	?

Junior holds

♠ xxx   ♡ AQxxx   ◇ xxx   ♣ xx

Pass. You have a definite right to assume that your partner's clubs are at least as strong as your hearts and, furthermore, you can see no game possibilities as your partner has not doubled.

The bidding:

Bidder	Senior	Responder	Junior
1 ♠	2 ♣	Pass	?

Junior holds

♠ x   ♡ AKxxx   ◇ xxx   ♣ Jxxx

Bid two hearts. With your favorable distribution there is
some possibility of game in hearts, and furthermore you
are prepared to raise Senior if he rebids.

The bidding:

Bidder	Senior	Responder	Junior
1 ♠	2 ♡	Pass	?

Junior holds

♠ Kx   ♡ Kxx   ◇ Axxx   ♣ Axxx

Bid two notrump. Senior's bid of two hearts shows either
a two-suited hand or a good heart suit. In the first instance

he will show his second suit over two notrump, whereupon you can safely bid four hearts. In the other case, he will rebid his hearts, whereupon you bid three notrump. If partner holds six hearts to the Ace-Queen, a spade lead up to your King would give you nine immediate tricks at notrump, while a spade lead through your King might easily defeat a four-heart contract.

> NOTE: *With a timid partner who would be un-likely to recognize the strong constructive nature of your two-notrump bid, it would be advisable to bid three notrump immediately over his two-heart overcall.*

The bidding:

Bidder	Senior	Responder	Junior
1 ♠	2 ♡	Pass	?

Junior holds

♠ A x x x   ♡ J x x   ◇ K Q J x x   ♣ x

Bid four hearts. It is an absolute certainty that your part-ner holds at least a good five- or six-card suit, which makes your three to the Jack adequate trump support, and with either first or second round control of all side suits a game seems likely.

The bidding:

Bidder	Senior	Responder	Junior
1 ◇	1 ♡	Pass	?

Junior holds

♠ A K x x x x   ♡ Q x x   ◇ x x   ♣ A x

Bid two spades. This bid is forcing to game and offers an eventual choice between spades and hearts.

NOTE: *This is another instance of a strong Jump bid by the Defending Side which is not to be confused with our immediate Jump Suit Overcall.*

ACTION BY JUNIOR AFTER RESPONDER BIDS OVER SENIOR'S OVERCALL

The first point for Junior to bear in mind is that the Opening bid has indicated a certain amount of strength, as has also the Free bid by Responder. Except in very rare instances, any action by Junior will be of a defensive nature and based mainly on distributional advantages.

Examples of action by Junior are:

The bidding:

Bidder	Senior	Responder	Junior
1 ♡	1 ♠	2 ♡	?

Junior holds

♠ Q x x x   ♡ x   ◇ Q x x x   ♣ x x x x

This is a worthless hand defensively. It appears almost certain that the opponents will reach a four-heart contract and it is imperative that you immediately inform your partner of a possible inexpensive defense at four spades. Accordingly, you should bid two spades.

The bidding:

Bidder	Senior	Responder	Junior
1 ♠	2 ◇	2 ♡	?

Junior holds

♠ x x x   ♡ A x x   ◇ A x x x   ♣ x x x

The presumption is that your partner's overcall is based on a long diamond suit, and that in spite of your two Aces,

there may be no defense against a final contract of either
four hearts or four spades. You immediately raise to
three diamonds to allow your partner to defend at five if
he desires.

CHAPTER XVI

Development of the Bidding After Senior's Attacking Calls

DEVELOPMENTS AFTER SENIOR'S ONE-NOTRUMP OVERCALL

As PREVIOUSLY pointed out, this bid indicates a hand fully as strong as an original one notrump. Senior may not be well prepared for a major suit response; otherwise he would probably double instead of bidding one notrump.

With this information Responder realizes that his side probably cannot score game if Senior's one-notrump overcall was sound. However, there is no guarantee that Senior's bid was not psychic or semi-psychic, and if Responder holds a good hand he should Double for business.

Any other bid by the Responder is probably a defensive measure. For instance, assume the bidding to have been one heart, one notrump by Senior, and Responder holds

$$\spadesuit \; Q\,J\,x\,x\,x\,x \qquad \heartsuit \; x \qquad \diamond \; Q\,x\,x \qquad \clubsuit \; x\,x$$

a two-spade bid is clearly indicated since it might discourage Junior from entering the bidding. Continuing the bidding around the table, suppose the Bidder held

$$\spadesuit \; x \qquad \heartsuit \; A\,K\,x\,x \qquad \diamond \; A\,x\,x\,x \qquad \clubsuit \; x\,x\,x$$

he should pass, realizing that Responder's two-spade bid indicated a long suit with few high cards.

In most instances the Responder will have to pass, thus putting the issue squarely up to Junior. His course of action in this case is not particularly difficult, however, since it is the same as if he were Responder and one no-trump had been the original bid.

DEVELOPMENT OF THE BIDDING AFTER A TAKEOUT DOUBLE BY SENIOR

The Takeout Double is the paradox among Bridge bids. While entirely artificial, in that it conveys a meaning diametrically opposite to that for which the Double was intended, namely, business; nevertheless, through constant usage its meaning is now clearly understood.

After a Takeout Double by Senior, the Attacking Side (the side which has opened the bidding) should completely modify and vary its tactics.

First, you (Responder) have the privilege of redoubling. This Redouble, which should be used as your principal strength-showing bid, is practically Forcing to game. It informs your partner that you have a fine hand and will be prepared to take action after the Redouble is taken out —as it surely will be. It enables you to catch the bluff doubler for an enormous penalty whenever his partner also has a weak hand; while in the event that the Bidder cares to continue to game or Slam, its use is a safeguard against interfering tactics by the opponents.

The next course of action that the Responder should consider is the pass. This may be made with a weak hand in which he can find no bid, but it may also be made with a good hand but one not quite strong enough for a Redouble. Bidder should definitely allow for the fact that when Responder passes a Double and subsequently enters the bidding, he is showing strength, whereas any immediate bid over the Double may deny it.

With this in mind, Responder, with a weak hand, can get in one defensive bid quickly, cheaply and safely. For instance, we have the one-notrump response. This indicates a balanced hand with some high card strength— about 4 or 5 points. Should Responder pass the Double and Junior then bid, Responder might never be able to show these few cards, but his bid, if made immediately, conveys certain, if meager, information to partner at a low and safe level of the contracting.

The bid of a new suit, in this instance, merely indicates a desire to play that suit in preference to the one bid by partner, and is not forcing.

Immediate Raises of partner's suit in this situation are similar to the Opening Pre-emptive bid in that they are purely defensive, and also overbids. Raises to two, three or four by Responder may be made with no high card strength whatsoever. If the bidding proceeds one spade, Double, four spades, Responder does not expect the Bidder to make his contract unless the Opening bid was very strong.

Similarly, Jump responses over the double in a new suit are not strength-showing, and are of a pre-emptive nature.

Examples of action by Responder are as follows:

♠ Q J x x x x   ♡ x   ◇ x x x   ♣ K x x

High card value 3½.

If Senior doubles your partner's Opening bid of one club, diamond or heart, you should bid one spade; while if Senior doubles your partner's Opening bid of one spade, you should Jump to three spades, if vulnerable, and to four spades, if not vulnerable.

♠ x x   ♡ x x   ◇ Q J 10 9 x x x   ♣ x x

High card value 1½.

If partner is doubled at one club, one heart or one spade, make a pre-emptive bid of three diamonds. Had one diamond been the doubled contract, you should attempt to shut out with four diamonds.

♠ x x   ♡ x x   ◇ Q J 10 9 x x   ♣ K x x

High card value 3½.

This hand represents a proper two-diamond Takeout over a doubled contract of one spade or one heart.

♠ Q J x x   ♡ x x   ◇ K Q x x   ♣ A x x

High card value 7½.

If the bidding is one spade, Double, the Responder should Redouble, as he surely wishes to reach game.

♠ J 10 x   ♡ x x   ◇ K x x x   ♣ K x x x

High card value 4½.

If partner's bid of one heart is doubled, Responder should bid one notrump. If partner's bid of one spade, one diamond or one club is doubled, Responder should give an immediate single Raise.

♠ Q x   ♡ K Q 10 x x   ◇ A x x   ♣ x x x

High card value 7.

If partner's opening bid is doubled we pass and await developments, intending to take subsequent action.

♠ x x x   ♡ x x   ◇ K x x x   ♣ Q x x x

High card value 3.

This hand is too weak for anything but a pass if a bid of one spade or one heart is doubled. However, we give a single Raise if the bid was one diamond or one club.

SUMMARY

In actual experience, the matter of action by Responder is one involving great difficulty. The shadings are so close that no one can always make the best choice. However, the student should bear in mind, first, that the Redouble is the strength-showing answer to bluff and weak Take-out Doubles; second, that immediate action is the proper procedure with a mediocre hand; and third, that the pass is made either with a blank hand or with one not quite strong enough to redouble, but with which we expect to be able to act later on.

ACTION BY JUNIOR AFTER SENIOR HAS DOUBLED

Junior's action depends upon what Responder has done. If Responder passes, Junior must respond to Senior's Double. It is absolutely inexcusable to pass in this situation unless you believe you can severely penalize the doubled contract. If Junior makes a Business Pass, his trump holding must be strong enough to stand having them opened by Senior. Remember, you cannot hurt a contract of one if the declarer can make his small trumps. Such holdings as Q J 10 9 x or even 10 9 8 7 x x are good enough for this purpose; A 5 4 3 2 or K J 8 6 3 are not.

The next least desirable action is the one-notrump response. Senior seeks some definite information about your hand, and the showing of a suit, even though weak, tells him more than one notrump. However, there are two instances where the notrump response is correct: first, when you cannot show a four-card suit other than the suit doubled; and second, when you have a balanced hand with a stopper or stoppers in the doubled suit and hope your partner will bid again so that you may support his suit or rebid in notrumps.

Experience has shown that it is rare indeed that the Doubler, himself, will not show a suit if his partner makes a one-notrump response to his Double. Now, if Junior's one-notrump response has been from weakness, he will, of course, pass, while if it has been from strength, he will bid again.

When Junior can respond in a suit, his problems are, first, which suit to choose, and second, whether his hand calls for a Jump response.

Here, our general rule is to bid a major in preference to a minor suit unless the disparity between the two is very great. Remember, as the Double by Senior has been an attacking measure, that it is better to launch the attack with a major suit than a minor.

Finally, Jump responses by Junior are forcing to game. We recommend that these Jump bids be used sparingly, and only when Junior not only has a fair hand, but also a good suit.

NOTE: *The Double has indicated a considerable amount of strength, and the reader will note from our examples that we frequently force after a Double by our partner with a hand which is below average in high cards, but which is strong in one or both major suits.*

Examples of action by Junior when Responder passes the Takeout Double:

The bidding is one spade, Double, pass, and Junior holds

♠ xxxx   ♡ xxx   ◇ xxx   ♣ Jxx

High card value ½.

Bid one notrump and pray.

The bidding is one spade, Double, pass, and Junior holds

♠ KJxx   ♡ Axx   ◇ xxx   ♣ Jxx

High card value 6.

Bid one notrump, intending to rebid if another bid is made.

♠ xx   ♡ xx   ◇ QJ1098   ♣ Axxx

High card value 4½.

Bid one diamond if a club has been doubled, or two diamonds if a spade or heart has been doubled. If one diamond has been doubled, pass for a penalty.

♠ KQ10xx   ♡ KJxx   ◇ xxx   ♣ x

High card value 5½.

If partner doubles a club, diamond or heart, bid two spades, a game-forcing bid. If one spade is doubled, bid two hearts—*do not pass.*

♠ AJxx   ♡ Axxx   ◇ xxx   ♣ xx

High card value 6½.

Bid only one spade over a Double of one heart, one diamond or one club, intending to take strong action if your partner bids again.

♠ 10 x x x   ♡ A x   ◊ K Q x x   ♣ x x x

High card value 6.

Bid one spade over a Double of one heart, one diamond or one club. If the Opening bid has been one club, this example illustrates our preference for a major-suit to a minor-suit response. Incidentally, with a five-card spade suit, this hand would be fully strong enough for a Jump response.

♠ x x   ♡ K x x x   ◊ A x x x x   ♣ x x

High card value 5.

If one spade is doubled, bid two hearts. If one club is doubled, bid one heart. From this it will be seen that we carry our preference for the major-suit response to the point of choosing a four-card major in preference to a five-card minor. However, it will be noted in this instance that we can conveniently show the diamond suit on our next bid.

♠ x   ♡ Q J 10 x x x x x   ◊ Q x   ♣ x x

High card value 2½.

Frequently, unusual hands call for unusual action. If partner doubles an Opening one-bid, we recommend an immediate Jump to four hearts. This bid indicates that we have a tremendous heart suit and at the same time denies any great high card strength because otherwise we would have made a simple Jump response, which would be forcing to game.

ACTION BY JUNIOR WHEN RESPONDER BIDS OVER
THE DOUBLE

In this situation there is no necessity for Junior to bid, as Responder has released him from his obligation. Therefore, a Free bid indicates some strength.

Some examples of action by Junior, when Responder bids, are:

The bidding is one spade, Double, two diamonds, and we hold

$$\spadesuit \text{ x x} \qquad \heartsuit \text{ Q J 10 x x} \qquad \diamondsuit \text{ x x} \qquad \clubsuit \text{ Q x x x}$$

High card value 2½.

Bid two hearts. If partner bids four, we shall probably make our contract.

The bidding is one heart, Double, one spade, and we hold

$$\spadesuit \text{ K J 10 x} \qquad \heartsuit \text{ x} \qquad \diamondsuit \text{ K x x x} \qquad \clubsuit \text{ x x x x}$$

High card value 4½.

Double. This is the best way to show our spade strength, and if Responder's bid has been psychic, it is immediately disclosed.

The bidding is one club, Double, four clubs, and we hold

$$\spadesuit \text{ K J 10 9 x} \qquad \heartsuit \text{ 10 x x} \qquad \diamondsuit \text{ x} \qquad \clubsuit \text{ x x x x}$$

High card value 2½.

Bid four spades. Our partner surely cannot have more than one club and must have good spade support. Furthermore, if we do not take action, it is probable that our partner will be shut out of the bidding. In this instance, as in all cases when the opponents pre-empt, our partner must realize that we may be overbidding in order to protect him.

ACTION BY JUNIOR OVER A REDOUBLE OF SENIOR'S DOUBLE OF A SUIT

In this position Junior is "on the spot." Most authorities have glossed over this subject in their books and as a result few know whether his pass indicates a desire to defeat the redoubled contract or merely an unwillingness to bid.

Our experience has shown us that a pass by Junior in this position should be used as a request to Senior to bid. The pass does not show a desire to play the redoubled contract. Once in a blue moon an opportunity to inflict a large penalty will be lost, but at all other times this procedure will secure the best results.

In some instances a bid by Junior may be the best course to pursue. For example, consider the following hand:

♠ x x ♡ J x x x ◇ x x x x ♣ x x x

The bidding is one club or one diamond, Double, Redouble. Although Junior has nothing, should he pass, Senior will probably bid one spade. Therefore, it behooves Junior to bid one heart to show the suit in which the least danger lurks. On the other hand, should the bidding be one spade, Double, Redouble, Junior should pass to allow Senior to elect his best suit as the rescue.

In order further to clarify this difficult situation we list below the different instances in which Junior should bid or pass:

A bid by Junior shows a *weak* hand and indicates:

(1) A five-card suit other than the one redoubled.

(2) A good four-card suit.

(3) Any four-card suit which can be bid at the level of one.

(4) Four or more cards of the suit redoubled with two probable stoppers. In this instance, he bids one notrump.

A pass by Junior would indicate one of the following hands:

(1) A weak hand with no five-card suit other than the one redoubled.

(2) A weak hand with no good four-card suit.

(3) A weak hand with no four-card suit which he can bid at the level of *one*.

(4) A strong hand with which he intends to enter the bidding later.

Examples of action by Junior over a Redouble:

♠ x x x   ♡ x x x   ◇ x x x   ♣ x x x x

With this hand we must pass the Redouble and let our partner take himself out. All suits, except clubs, look equally undesirable to us, and even clubs do not particularly please us.

♠ x x   ♡ x x x   ◇ x x x   ♣ x x x x x

If the redoubled bid is one club, we pass, permitting partner to choose his own suit. If any other redoubled bid comes to us, we bid two clubs.

♠ x x   ♡ x x x x   ◇ x x x   ♣ x x x x

With this hand we bid one heart over a redoubled diamond or club, but pass a redoubled spade.

♠ A x x   ♡ x x x x   ◇ A x x   ♣ K x x

This hand is an example of the strong pass. Obviously, one of the three bids is psychic—probably the Redouble. Of course, we are prepared to take strong action at our next turn to bid.

♠ x x x   ♡ x x   ◇ K J 10 x   ♣ x x x x

This hand includes a good four-card suit and we bid one diamond over a redoubled club, two diamonds over a redoubled heart or spade, or one notrump over a redoubled diamond.

♠ x x x x   ♡ x x   ◇ K J 10 x   ♣ x x x

Here we have a weak four-card spade suit and a good four-card diamond suit. Over one club, redoubled, we bid one diamond, but over one heart, redoubled, we bid one spade. Over one diamond, redoubled, we, similarly, prefer one spade to one notrump, but over one spade, redoubled, we bid two diamonds.

SECOND ROUND ACTION BY SENIOR AFTER HE HAS MADE A TAKEOUT DOUBLE

If Responder bids over the Double, Junior may pass, as he has been relieved from his obligation to bid. Senior may double again after the original Bidder has acted, as a further request to Junior to bid. Repeated Doubles, of course, indicate greater strength.

If Junior bids freely after Responder has bid, he (Junior) is marked with some strength, and Senior should take this into account in his subsequent bidding.

If Responder passes, Junior's response is forced and may be made on an utterly worthless hand. In considering a rebid Senior should realize this, and, therefore, any strong action by Senior must be based on a very powerful hand.

The following are examples:

♠ A K x x x   ♡ A x x x   ◇ x x   ♣ K x

High card value 10.

Bidding:

Bidder	Senior	Responder	Junior
1 ◇	Double	Pass	1 ♠

Senior should bid two spades. To make game, Junior must be able to make a further bid. Similarly, should Junior's response be one heart, a Raise to two would be sufficient.

If Junior should respond with one notrump or two clubs, we recommend a two-spade bid.

♠ K Q J x x x   ♡ x   ◇ A x x   ♣ A x x

High card value 9½.

This is an example of a one-suit Double, which requires some positive action by partner before we can attempt game. Should partner's response to our Double be one spade, we bid two spades only, while a response in another suit would merely necessitate a minimum bid of spades on our part. However, any second bid by Junior, would encourage us, and we would make a game bid.

♠ K Q x x   ♡ K Q x x   ◇ A K x x   ♣ x

High card value 11.

After doubling a club or diamond bid, we jump our partner's one-spade or one-heart response to three.

SUMMARY OF ACTION AFTER A TAKEOUT DOUBLE

There are certain guiding principles to bear in mind:

First, the Takeout Double by Senior should be an attacking measure.

Second, Responder with a fine hand, should redouble to inform the Bidder that he is prepared to continue the attack or to double the opponents; with a good hand, Responder should pass to await developments; but with only a fair hand, he should act immediately, to avoid the danger of being shut out; with a bad hand, he should pass.

Third, Junior should realize that a Takeout Double is a request for a *suit* response and should endeavor to find such a bid.

Fourth, having made a simple response, Junior should realize that any Jump bid in a new suit by the Doubler is the *strongest* kind of Qualified Force. For instance, should Junior hold

♠ x x x x   ♡ J 10 x   ◇ x x x x   ♣ x x

and the bidding be

Bidder	Senior	Responder	Junior
1 ◇	Double	Pass	1 ♠
Pass	3 ♡	Pass	?

he should bid four hearts, as his three trumps to the Jack-ten, combined with the doubleton club, should be worth one and possibly two tricks to Senior, who might hold a hand such as the following:

♠ A x   ♡ A K x x x x   ◇ x   ♣ A K x x

CHAPTER XVII

Defensive Bidding After an Opening One-Notrump Bid

ACTION BY SENIOR

IN ACCORDANCE with the Principle of Risk versus Gain, Senior should pass an Opening notrump in nearly all instances. As Senior will have the lead, his best policy is to try to defeat whatever number of notrumps becomes the eventual contract, rather than endeavor to make the eight or more tricks necessary to fulfill a contract of his own.

Senior should overcall only when his hand is strong in playing strength (the Limit of Risk is two tricks, vulnerable, or three tricks, not vulnerable), and when his defense against notrump appears to be slight. If he has a very strong hand, he should double for *business*.

This procedure is contrary to that recommended over an Opening bid of one of a suit. The reason why we double one notrump for business lies in the fact that if we can make game against an Opening one notrump, we can probably penalize the opponents more than the value of game, particularly as we have the advantage of the opening lead.*

In order to double a notrump, it is not necessary for

---

* In general, the opening lead is an advantage against notrump.

Senior to have the set in his own hand. However, he should expect to take at least six tricks.

Junior should always pass this Double with a balanced hand, regardless of strength, but may take out when he has a weak hand with a long suit.

Some examples of action by Senior over an Opening bid of one notrump are:

♠ A x x   ♡ K x x   ◇ K x x   ♣ Q J x x

High card value 8½.

Pass. The hand is weaker than the Opening one-notrump, hence, there is no point in doubling or otherwise entering the bidding.

♠ A K Q J x x   ♡ x x   ◇ x x x   ♣ K x

High card value 8½.

Pass. An immediate spade overcall would warn the opponents away from notrump. Furthermore, if Responder bids a suit, we will have an opportunity to bid spades on the second round.

♠ Q J 10 9 x x   ♡ K Q 10 x   ◇ x   ♣ x x

High card value 4½.

Bid two spades. This bid cannot be penalized severely and may keep the opponents from a three-notrump contract.

♠ K 8 5 4 3 2   ♡ A   ◇ K 5 3   ♣ 8 6 4

High card value 7.

Pass. A two-spade overcall might easily be set four tricks.

♠ K Q J x x   ♡ A Q   ◇ K x x   ♣ A x x

High card value 12½.

Double.

♠ A K x   ♡ A Q x   ◇ K Q J x   ♣ Q J x

High card value 14.

Double.

ACTION BY JUNIOR AFTER SENIOR PASSES A ONE-NOTRUMP BID

If Responder also passes, Junior realizes that the Attacking side believes it has no game. However, Bidder may have a sound notrump, and Responder slightly less than the requirements for a Raise. Therefore, Junior cannot exercise the same freedom in reopening the bidding as he can when Responder passes a one-bid in a suit.

On the other hand, he is entitled to mark Senior with some strength and may overcall slightly more freely than Senior would be able to; a Double by Junior is made in the hope that Senior will have enough strength to make a Business Pass. If Senior holds a count of about 5 (two Kings and a Queen), or a fair five-card suit (Q 10 x x x) and one sure re-entry, he should pass and expect a penalty.

Some examples of action by Junior after Senior and Responder pass are:

♠ K Q J 10 x x   ♡ x x   ◇ x x x   ♣ x x

High card value 3½.

Bid two spades.

♠ A x x   ♡ K 10 x   ◇ Q x x   ♣ K J x x

High card value 8½.

Double, hoping partner will leave it in. If he takes out, you have support for his suit.

♠ x   ♡ K x x x x   ◇ Q x x x   ♣ A J x

High card value 6½.

Pass. Some players would be tempted to bid two hearts with this hand. To do so would probably lead to trouble, particularly if the Opening notrump was strong and Responder had almost enough to raise. *There is seldom anything to be gained by bidding weak suits against an Opening notrump bid.*

ACTION BY JUNIOR AFTER RESPONDER BIDS

Except in rare instances when the Opening notrump was purely psychic or when Junior has a tremendous freak, any action by Junior in this situation must be defensive and in the nature of a Lead-directing bid. Furthermore, and most important, Junior should bear in mind that any bid by him at this point probably will be doubled. Consequently, to justify a bid his hand should be strong enough (assuming Senior holds a bust) to insure against a set of more than two tricks, vulnerable, and three tricks, not vulnerable.

CHAPTER XVIII

Action Over a Pre-emptive Bid

WE MAKE extensive use of Pre-emptive bids as a part of the Four Aces System because up to the present time no satisfactory method of coping with them has been developed. After an Opening Pre-emptive bid, Senior and Junior cannot exchange information in a normal logical manner. Frequently, in order to enter the bidding, they must exceed the normal Limit of Risk to the extent of perhaps a four-trick penalty.

If either enters the bidding, his partner cannot know if his bid is sound or speculative. Furthermore, it must be borne in mind that although the Opening Pre-emptive bid indicates that Bidder has a weak hand, it gives no key either to the high card strength or distribution of *Responder*. If the opponents enter the bidding, they are quite likely to find the trumps bunched against them in Responder's hand.

The bidding against a Pre-emptive bid of three is substantially different from that against one of four. The Double of an Opening three-bid is primarily for a Takeout; while the Double of an Opening four-bid is primarily for business.

If, after an Opening four-bid, a player, with a very fine hand, wishes to force his partner to select a suit, he may do so by a bid of four notrump. After an Opening three-bid, however, a bid of *three notrump indicates a desire to play the hand at that contract.*

As these distinctions are very important, it is absolutely necessary when your opponents pre-empt that you and your partner have a clear understanding of what your bids mean. In few situations is a misunderstanding likely to be more costly.

In most instances when a Pre-emptive bid is made, Responder will take no action. When he does, beware, because he probably has a very fine hand.

Examples of action by Senior and Junior after an Opening Pre-emptive bid:

♠ A K 10 8 6 3   ♡ x   ◇ A K x x   ♣ x x

High card value 10.

Following an Opening Pre-emptive bid of four hearts or four clubs, Senior must risk a bid of four spades whether vulnerable or not. While there is a slight chance that he may be penalized severely at a four-spade contract, he should not allow himself to be shut out of the bidding with this very fine hand. Over three clubs or three hearts, he should bid only three spades.

Should Junior hold this hand, he would take the same action as Senior but with somewhat less risk, as the trumps, if bunched against him, would be in Responder's hand (under him).

♠ K J 9 x x   ♡ x   ◇ K x x   ♣ Q x x x

High card value 5½.

Senior cannot afford to take any action over any Pre-emptive bid except that he should double four spades. An Opening three-heart bid would tempt a foolhardy player to overcall, but he should bear in mind that all he holds, in addition to his split five-card suit, is a King and a Queen, and that unless Junior has a strong hand, a bid of three spades might be badly punished.

♠ A x   ♡ A x x   ◇ K Q x x   ♣ K x x x

High card value 11.

With this hand Senior should double any Opening four-bid. A bid of three spades or three hearts leaves him in an impossible situation, since any positive action might result in a large penalty. Probably he had best say to himself, "I hope there is more bidding," and pass.

♠ K x   ♡ A x   ◇ A K Q J x x   ♣ x x x

High card value 11½.

Senior should bid three notrump over an Opening three-spade or three-heart bid. After an Opening four-spade or four-heart bid, he may double, or bid five diamonds, the choice being an absolute guess.

♠ K Q x   ♡ A K x   ◇ A K x   ♣ K x x x

High card value 15.

Three notrump must be bid with this hand over any Opening three-bid.

♠ K x x   ♡ x x   ◇ A x x x   ♣ A x x x

High card value 8.

Any Opening Pre-emptive bid shuts out the holder of this hand. We do not recommend doubling an Opening four-bid.

♠ K J x x   ♡ x   ◇ A x x x   ♣ A x x x

High card value 8½.

With this hand, you should double an Opening three-heart bid for a Takeout.

♠ A K J 10 x x   ♡ x   ◇ K Q x x   ♣ K x

High card value 10½.

Bid four spades over any Opening Pre-emptive bid. Over an Opening three-bid, it is a Jump and is equivalent to saying: "Partner, I am too strong to take any chance of not reaching game."

♠ A K Q J 10 9 x x   ♡ x x   ◇ x x   ♣ x

High card value 6½.

Bid only three spades over an Opening Pre-emptive bid of three. Since the Pre-emptive bid is weak in high cards, there surely will be plenty of further action, and there is no point in hurrying the bidding.

♠ x   ♡ A K x x   ◇ K Q J x   ♣ A K x x

High card value 13½.

Double an Opening three-spade bid for a Takeout, and bid four notrump for a Takeout over an Opening four-spade bid.

CHAPTER XIX

Other Competitive Situations After an Opening Bid of One of a Suit

THE number of such situations is legion. However, let us consider those which are readily classified:

1. The Rebid when Senior and Responder pass and Junior reopens.
2. The Rebid when Senior overcalls and Responder passes.
3. The Free rebid and the Forcing Pass by the Attacking Side.
4. General principles applying to competitive situations in the higher stages of the bidding, including Business Doubles by either side.

THE REBID WHEN SENIOR AND RESPONDER PASS AND JUNIOR REOPENS

At this point the Bidder must realize the ominous significance of partner's pass. The Bidder has no right to count on Responder for either high cards or trump support, and any rebids must be based solely on his own taking tricks. Furthermore, in this situation, unlike other defensive situations, the Limit of Risk should be lowered to one trick, vulnerable, and two tricks, not vulnerable.

Examples of action in this situation are as follows:

♠ K Q J 10 9 x   ♡ A x x   ◇ A x x   ♣ x

High card value 9½.

The bidding has been one spade, pass, pass, and Junior reopens either by doubling or by bidding two of another suit. Whichever action Junior takes, the Bidder may properly rebid to two spades, as he cannot be set more than one trick, and the rebid may make it more difficult for his opponents to reach the best final contract. The reader will note that this hand, while strong in playing strength, includes, at most, three defensive tricks against an adverse suit contract.

♠ A Q x x   ♡ A Q x x   ◇ x x   ♣ A K x

High card value 13.

The bidding has been one spade, pass, pass, and Junior reopens with two diamonds. Here you must pass. Your high card strength is such that you fear no adverse game. On the other hand, your playing strength is not great and to rebid would be dangerous.

♠ A K x x x   ♡ A K x x x   ◇ x x   ♣ x

High card value 10.

The opening bid of one spade is followed by two passes, and Junior reopens with two diamonds or two clubs. Bid two hearts, as the risk of a penalty is not great and this strong two-suiter even shows game possibilities if Responder has some such holding as five hearts and a doubleton spade.

♠ K Q J x   ♡ A K J x   ◇ A Q 10 x   ♣ x

High card value 13.

Junior reopens with two clubs over our opening spade bid. Bidder should double, inviting Responder to show a suit or to pass if long in clubs.

THE REBID WHEN SENIOR OVERCALLS AND RESPONDER PASSES

This presents an entirely different situation, as Responder's pass indicates only that the maximum strength of his hand is insufficient for a Free bid. It does not necessarily mean that he could not have bid after a pass by Senior.

Let us consider example hands:

♠ K Q J 10 9 x   ♡ A x x   ◇ A x x   ♣ x

High card value 9½.

Senior overcalls our one spade with a bid of two in another suit and Responder and Junior pass. This situation calls for a rebid of two spades.

Suppose that Senior has overcalled with two hearts and Junior has raised to three hearts. Now we must bid three spades. This bid shows the full strength of our hand. Any further action must be taken by our partner.

♠ A Q x x   ♡ A Q x x   ◇ x x   ♣ A K x

High card value 13.

The bidding has been: one spade, two diamonds, pass, pass. This situation calls for a Takeout Double.* After all, if Responder has nothing but five hearts to the King,

---

* The Double in this instance is quite different from the Double of an Opening bid of one of a suit; when Senior doubles one of a suit, he is practically commanding his partner to take out; when Bidder doubles Senior's overcall, he is willing to have the Double left in if Responder holds trump strength in back of the declarer.

he will have a play for four hearts. Furthermore, should Responder have diamond strength (back of Senior) he can pass our Takeout Double.

♠ A K Q J x x   ♡ A x x   ◇ x   ♣ K Q x

High card value 12½.

The bidding:

Bidder	Senior	Responder	Junior
1 ♠	2 ◇	Pass	Pass

Make a Jump three-spade bid, strongly inviting game. We do not double in this situation as we do not want partner to leave it in.

♠ K Q J x x   ♡ K Q J x x   ◇ x   ♣ A x

High card value 10.

The bidding:

Bidder	Senior	Responder	Junior
1 ♠	2 ◇	Pass	Pass

Bid three hearts—another strong game invitation.

♠ K Q J x x x x   ♡ A Q J x   ◇ x   ♣ —

High card value 8.

The bidding:

Bidder	Senior	Responder	Junior
1 ♠	2 ◇	Pass	Pass

Bid four spades! A game in spades is certain.*

* Four spades should not be bid originally as the hand has great **Slam** possibilities.

♠ A K x x x   ♡ A K x x x   ◇ x x   ♣ x

High card value 10.

The bidding has gone one spade, two clubs or two diamonds by Senior, and Responder has passed. Bid two hearts if Junior passes; if Junior raises Senior's bid to three, bid three hearts.

THE FORCING PASS AND THE FREE REBID

The Forcing Pass occurs when a player who has previously made one or more strong bids passes an obvious defensive bid by an opponent because he wishes his partner to decide whether to bid more or to double. For instance, the bidding proceeds:

Bidder	Senior	Responder	Junior
1 ♡	Pass	3 ♡	4 ♣
4 ♡	5 ♣	Pass	

Here the pass by Responder merely indicates that he wishes to give Bidder a choice between doubling and bidding five hearts.

The fo!!owing would also be a Forcing Pass:

Bidder	Senior	Responder	Junior
1 ♠	2 ♡	2 ♠	3 ♡
4 ♠	Pass	Pass	5 ♡
Pass			

Consider this bidding:

Bidder	Senior	Responder	Junior
1 ♡	Pass	3 ♡	4 ♣
4 ♡			

Had there been no four-club bid, four hearts would have

been a mere response to the Force, but the four-club bid removed the necessity for Bidder to respond to the Force, and with a minimum hand he might well have passed. Therefore, the four-heart call was a Free rebid and showed additional values. A pass of the four clubs would be a Forcing Pass, as the Jump to three hearts was a guarantee that the bidding would proceed to game.

In many instances, failure to make a Free rebid is not forcing. For example:

Bidder	Senior	Responder	Junior
1 ♣	Pass	1 ♡	1 ♠
Pass			

The failure to make a Free rebid merely indicates that the one-club bid was a minimum. The partnership has not as yet shown that it has the preponderance of strength.

GENERAL PRINCIPLES APPLYING TO COMPETITIVE SITUA-
TIONS IN THE HIGHER STAGES OF THE BIDDING

(A) *Problems of the side which knows or at least believes that it is defending.*

Except in the rare case when you are considering defense against a probable or actual Slam contract, you should endeavor to keep your Limit of Risk *below* the value of the game which the Attacking Side may score. Any risk whatsoever is tactically unsound when you have a fair chance of defeating the adverse contract.

The following hands are examples of proper defensive procedure:

Example 1. Neither side vulnerable, you are Senior and hold

♠ K Q J x x x   ♡ x   ◇ Q J 10 x   ♣ x x

High card value 5.

Bidding (a):

Bidder	Senior	Responder	Junior
1 ♡	1 ♠	2 ♡	2 ♠
4 ♡	?		

Bid four spades. Your hand not only offers practically no defense against the four-heart contract, but you may have an outside chance of making your contract; in any event, the penalty should be less than the value of the adverse game.

Bidding (b):

Bidder	Senior	Responder	Junior
1 ♡	1 ♠	2 ♡	2 ♠
3 ♡	?		

Bid three spades. A pass in this situation would be based on tactics similar to those employed by the ostrich; when danger threatens, it buries its head in the sand to hide itself from its enemy. If Responder has a good hand, he will bid four hearts whether or not you bid three spades; while if you pass and he has a weak hand and passes, you will have lost the chance to play the hand at three spades. Furthermore, if Junior can bid four spades freely, you should be able to make it.

Example 2. Neither side vulnerable, you are Junior and hold

♠ A 10 x x   ♡ Q x x   ◇ A x x x   ♣ J x

High card value 7½.

Bidding (a):

Bidder	Senior	Responder	Junior
1 ♡	1 ♠	2 ♡	2 ♠
3 ♡	Pass	4 ♡	?

Pass. Your partner's failure to rebid has indicated that you will have no play for four spades. On the other hand, with your holding plus the slight strength shown by Senior's overcall, there is a fair chance of defeating the four-heart contract.

Bidding (b) or (c):

Bidder	Senior	Responder	Junior
1 ♡	1 ♠	2 ♡	2 ♠
3 ♡	3 ♠	4 ♡	?

or

1 ♡	1 ♠	2 ♡	2 ♠
3 ♡	3 ♠	Pass	?

Bid four spades. Whether Responder has bid four hearts or not makes no difference; after Senior's rebid you should play the hand at an attacking four-spade contract.

(B) *Problems of the Attacking Side.*

Problems encountered in attacking bidding are among the most difficult that face the Bridge player. The question is whether to bid, double, or make a Forcing Pass.

In such situations, when your hand clearly calls for a further bid, make it; when it clearly calls for a Double of the opponents, double them. If you are in doubt as to your proper course of action, make the Forcing Pass, and leave the decision to your partner. For instance, consider the following situation, neither side vulnerable:

The bidding:

Bidder	Senior	Responder	Junior
1 ♠	2 ♡	2 ♠	3 ♡
4 ♠	5 ♡	?	

Obviously, the five-heart bid is defensive. Most players in Responder's position consider only two choices of action, namely: whether to bid five spades or to double. Actually, there is a third choice, the Forcing Pass.

In the event that you double you are implying: (1) "Partner, we can defeat this contract of five hearts for an amount equivalent to, or more than, making five spades would give us, or, (2) Partner, I do not think we can make five spades, but I know we can defeat five hearts."

If you make a Forcing Pass, you tell your partner that your hand is of such nature that you expect him to bid five spades if his previous bidding has been based largely on distribution, and to double if it has been based on high cards.

Five spades should not be bid unless you are practically certain that it can be made.

After an Opening one-spade by partner, the following hands all demand a Free Raise to two spades as your first response. Nevertheless, each calls for different action after the opponents have reached five hearts on the bidding shown above.

♠ A x x   ♡ K x x x   ◊ Q x x x x   ♣ x

High card value 6.

Double. There is a fine chance of severely penalizing the five-heart bid, while due to the fact that you have only three trumps, it is quite likely that your partner cannot make five spades.

♠ Qxxxx ♡ x ◇ Axxxx ♣ xx

High card value 4.

Bid five spades. You should have a good chance of making this contract, and you certainly cannot hurt the opponents at five hearts.

♠ Kxxx ♡ xxx ◇ AQxx ♣ xx

High card value 6.

Here your best course is to make a Forcing Pass. If your partner has reason to believe he can make five spades he will bid it; otherwise, he will double.

(C) *Problems when it is doubtful as to which side is defending.*

The problems arising in this situation are similar to those under B, except that now a pass is not forcing, and may be made merely because the player is not strong enough to double or to bid more. For example, consider the following bidding:

Bidder	Senior	Responder	Junior
1 ♡	1 ♠	2 ♣	2 ♠
Pass	3 ♠	4 ♣	4 ♠
Pass			

In this instance, the pass by the original Bidder is in no manner forcing. It confirms the fact that he has a minimum bid and furthermore sees no clearly indicated course of action.

While this example has been given without an illustrative hand, its main purpose is to introduce the subject of the use (or the misuse, as is generally the case) of the Double, made purely to stop your partner from bidding.

It is obvious that in a competitive situation any Double must carry with it a request to your partner to bid no more; nevertheless, the fact that you do not double should not be read as an invitation to your partner to continue. However, while we positively do not recommend its use simply to stop partner from bidding, there are occasional instances when you may make a close Double because you greatly fear bad results should your partner continue. For example, both sides have 90 on score. You are Senior, and the bidding proceeds:

Bidder	Senior	Responder	Junior
1 ♡	Pass	Pass	1 ♠
2 ♡	Pass	Pass	2 ♠
3 ♡	Pass	Pass	3 ♠
4 ♡	?		

You hold

♠ x   ♡ Q x x x   ◇ x x x x   ♣ x x x x

High card value 1.

While this hand is completely worthless in support of your partner's spades, it contains at least one sure defensive trick against four hearts, and, therefore, there is a distinct probability of defeating the four-heart contract. It follows that you should double.

CHAPTER XX

Business Doubles of Non-Competitive Contracts

MOST players are inclined to double their opponents' game and Slam contracts too freely. In doing so they expose themselves to Redoubles and enormous bonuses for over-tricks—remember, there is no such thing as a *Free* Double. On the other hand, there are some who do not double often enough and permit reckless overbidding to go un-punished.

The proper course is midway between these two ex-tremes. The player, who boasts that no one can make a contract when he has doubled, does not double often enough; the player, who finds that one doubled contract out of three is being made, doubles too often.

Before making a Penalty Double, be sure there is a definite and sound reason for the move. If certain of set-ting the opponents, double, even though it may be for but one trick; if at all doubtful do not double unless there is a possibility of beating them several tricks. In doubling, be very careful that the information imparted to declarer by your Double does not enable him to make his contract. *Finally, do not double with the expectation of picking up tricks in partner's hand when he has not bid.*

The following are examples of proper and improper Doubles:

♠ x x x   ♡ A x x   ♣ A x x x   ◇ A x x

High card value 9.

The bidding:

Bidder	Senior	Responder	Junior
1 ♠	Pass	2 ◇	Pass
2 ♣	Pass	3 ♠	Pass
4 ♠	?		

A Double by Senior would be very bad. Although the opponents have not shown unusual strength, and are missing three Aces, their bidding has at all times been constructive. Therefore, it is almost a certainty that both are well stocked with Kings, Queens, and short suits. It would be very unreasonable to expect Junior to take more than one trick, and it is likely that he will take none. Finally, the ghastly specter of the Redouble may be stalking in the background waiting for his victim and if the dreaded creature suddenly appears and strikes, the damage would be out of all proportion to the possible gain.

♠ Q J 10 x   ♡ A x   ◇ A x   ♣ J 10 9 8 7

High card value 8.

The bidding:

Bidder	Senior	Responder	Junior
1 ♠	Pass	3 ♠	Pass
4 ♠	Double		

Here we know that the opponents are unaware of the bad trump distribution, else they would not have bid to game so confidently. We are certain of setting the contract at least one trick without any assistance whatsoever from partner.

♠ Q 10 x x   ♡ A x x   ◇ A x x   ♣ x x x

High card value 7.

The bidding:

Bidder	Senior	Responder	Junior
1 ♠	Pass	3 ♠	Pass
4 ♠	?		

We have reason to believe that four spades cannot be made against our hand. On the other hand, a Double would give the declarer a clue to our holding and might enable him to make the hand by playing it from the start, on the assumption that we hold four trumps to the Queen-ten. A rule which applies to all Business Doubles may be stated as follows: *Never double when by so doing you jeopardize the setting trick.*

♠ K x x   ♡ K x x   ◇ J 10 9 x x   ♣ x x

High card value 4½.

The bidding:

Bidder	Senior	Responder	Junior
2 N T	Pass	3 ♣	Pass
3 N T	Pass	4 N T	Pass
6 N T	?		

It is reasonable to assume that both your Kings will lie in back of the declarer's Aces, and that should he finesse against them, you will set the contract one trick. However, declarer may be able to make enough tricks in the minor suits and in one of the two majors to fulfill his Slam contract. If he cannot do so he may correctly reason that your Double is based on both Kings, and instead of finessing work out a successful end play against you. You should pass.

♠ K J x   ♡ x x x   ◇ A Q x x   ♣ A x x

High card value 9½.

The bidding:

Bidder	Senior	Responder	You
1 ♡	Pass	1 ♠	Pass
2 ♡	Pass	3 ♣	Pass
3 N T	?		

Pass. The Bidder's rebid of hearts shows a strong suit—possibly one of six cards—while Responder has not only bid two suits, missing the King-Jack of one and the Ace of the other, but has bid his second suit as a Skip Level Shift. Our King-Jack of spades probably lie under the Ace-Queen, while any honors our partner may have in hearts are under declarer's strong suit. Finally, although we probably hold the Ace-Queen of diamonds over the King, it is extremely unlikely that our partner will have the opportunity of leading through it.

THE FOUR ACES' LEAD-DIRECTING DOUBLE

As a rule, a Double merely indicates that you can defeat the contract and wish to increase the penalty bonus. However, against three-notrump or a Slam contract, experience has shown that best results are obtained if the Double by the player not on lead is made for lead-directing purposes. Therefore, we present the Four Aces Lead-directing Double Convention.

Case 1. The Double of Three Notrump by the Player Not on Lead.

(a) Neither you nor your partner has bid. In this case your Double is a definite request to your partner to lead the first suit bid by Dummy. For example:

Bidder	Senior	Responder	You
1 ♠	Pass	2 ♢	Pass
2 N T	Pass	3 N T	*Double*

You hold the following hand:

♠ A x x   ♡ A x x   ♢ Q J 10 9 7   ♣ x x

In this situation you are asking for a diamond lead, and almost surely will set the contract with that lead. Only by means of this convention can you get the lead you desire.

(b) When you have bid a suit yourself. In this instance your Double tells your partner to lead your suit. For example:

Bidder	Senior	Responder	You
1 ♢	Pass	1 ♡	1 ♠
1 N T	Pass	2 N T	Pass
3 N T	Pass	Pass	*Double*

You hold the following hand:

♠ K Q J 10 x   ♡ x x x x   ♢ A x x   ♣ x

This Double definitely demands a spade lead. Without a spade lead, you believe that the contract will be made; with a spade lead you expect to defeat the contract.

It is worthy of note in connection with this hand that your partner might hold

♠ x ♡ xxx ◇ xxx ♣ K Q 10 9 xx

Without this convention, he would certainly open a club and the contract would be made.

(c) When you have not bid, but your partner has. In this instance your Double asks your partner to lead his suit. For example:

Bidder	Senior	Responder	You
1 ♣	1 ♠	2 ◇	Pass
2 N T	Pass	3 N T	*Double*

You hold the following hand:

♠ K x x ♡ x x ◇ A x x x ♣ J 10 x x

You believe that a spade lead will defeat the contract, and fear that if you do not make this Lead-directing Double, your partner will open some other suit.

Case 2. *The Double of a Slam Contract by the Player Not on Lead.*

Against ordinary contracts, the primary purpose of a Double is to penalize an overbid as much as possible; against a Slam contract, the primary purpose is to convey information to partner which will enable him to make the lead most likely to defeat the contract. Therefore, in the Four Aces System, the Double of a Slam bid is always a request for a specific lead.

The lead requested depends upon the bidding. In the event that Dummy has bid any suit or suits other than the final trump, our Double demands a lead of the first suit bid by Dummy. In the event that Dummy has bid no side suits, but declarer has, our Double demands a lead of the first side suit bid by declarer. In the event that neither

Dummy nor declarer has bid any side suits, but our side has, the Double demands a lead of one of the *unbid* suits. This rare case is the only time when the leader must make a decision.

In view of this specific doubling convention, you must not double a Slam when you want a normal lead except when your hand is so strong that you will certainly set the contract irrespective of the opening. You may occasionally lose an opportunity to gather in an extra fifty or hundred points, but you will defeat many otherwise makable Slams.

The following are examples of Lead-directing Doubles against a Slam:

Bidder	Senior	Responder	You
1 ♡	Pass	2 ◇	Pass
3 ♡	Pass	4 ♡	Pass
5 ♣	Pass	6 ♡	*Double*

You hold the following hand:

♠ A x x x x   ♡ x x x   ◇ —   ♣ x x x x x

In this instance the Lead-directing Double calls for a diamond lead, the first and only suit bid by Dummy. You will trump this lead, and now if your spade Ace holds, you will defeat the contract.

Bidder	Senior	Responder	You
1 ♣	Pass	1 ◇	Pass
2 ♣	Pass	4 ♣	Pass
6 ♣	Pass	Pass	*Pass*

You hold the following hand:

♠ J x x x   ♡ A x x   ◇ x x x   ♣ Q J 10

While you are almost certain of defeating six-clubs,

you do not double, since your Double would request a
diamond opening, which might enable the opponents to
make the contract. You cheerfully give up the additional
fifty or hundred points that a Double might bring you—
Slams should not be doubled to gain trifles.

Bidder	Senior	Responder	You
1 ♣	Pass	3 ♣	3 ♠
6 ♣	Pass	Pass	Double

You hold the following hand:

♠ J 10 9 x x x x   ♡ A x x   ◊ A x   ♣ x

You do not want a spade lead even though you bid the
suit at the level of three. Your Double demands a heart
or diamond opening; a spade lead might permit declarer
to make his contract.

Bidder	You	Responder	Junior
1 ♡	3 ♠	4 ◊	Pass
4 ♠	Pass	5 ♣	Pass
6 ◊	Pass	7 ◊	Pass
Pass	Double		

You hold the following hand:

♠ A Q J 10 x x x   ♡ —   ◊ x x   ♣ Q x x x

The Double demands a heart lead, the first side suit bid
by Dummy. If the opponents have bid correctly, this is
the only lead to defeat the Grand Slam contract.

Bidder	Senior	Responder	Junior
1 ♡	Pass	2 ◊	Pass
6 ♡	Pass	Pass	Double

In this case, the Double can call for but one lead—a

diamond. While this bidding is of course very unusual, it actually took place among four expert players on the following deal:

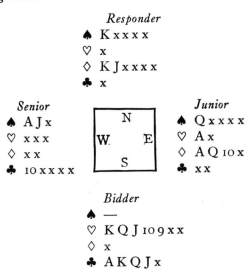

Responder
♠ K x x x x
♡ x
◇ K J x x x x
♣ x

Senior
♠ A J x
♡ x x x
◇ x x
♣ 10 x x x x

N
W E
S

Junior
♠ Q x x x x
♡ A x
◇ A Q 10 x
♣ x x

Bidder
♠ —
♡ K Q J 10 9 x x
◇ x
♣ A K Q J x

Senior was so surprised at the Double that he ignored his partner's command and opened the Ace of spades, whereupon the declarer ruffed in his own hand, led the Ace of clubs, ruffed a low club, discarded his losing diamond on the King of spades, ruffed back into his own hand, and then drew trumps, making the six-heart contract. If the command of the lead-directing Double had been followed, the contract would have been set two tricks.

CHAPTER XXI

Slam Bidding

INTRODUCTION

It has been customary in books on Bridge to treat Slam bidding as separate and distinct from game bidding. As a result, many readers have gained the impression that they are also separate and distinct in principle. This impression, however, is erroneous, as the two subjects are closely related. We wish to emphasize the fact that the groundwork for successful Slam bidding is laid below the game level.

Slam bonuses are so large that the use of unsuccessful methods in Slam bidding may make an otherwise fine player a loser, while successful Slam bidding will often make the otherwise mediocre player a winner. Mathematically, when you proceed from game to a Small Slam you risk an amount approximately equal to the Slam bonus. When you proceed from a Small Slam to a Grand Slam, you risk an amount approximately equal to twice the difference between the Small and Grand Slam bonuses. Therefore, in accordance with the Principle of Risk versus Gain, a Small Slam should be bid only when it offers better than an even chance of success; a Grand Slam, only when it offers better than a two-to-one chance.

While contracts of one less than game are undesirable,

final contracts of more than game and less than a Slam are anathema.* When you make this bid and go down one, you have thrown away a game. When you make your contract, you receive no greater bonus than if you had stopped at game. This thought will help to emphasize our first rule for Slam bidding: Always endeavor to sound out Slam possibilities at or below the game level and reserve bids of more than game as almost Slam commands.

After the Opening bid, Responder, with a good hand, should always visualize a Slam possibility. Following the Principle of Anticipation when selecting his response, he should say to himself: "If partner does so and so, then I intend either to invite or bid a Slam."

If the Opening Bidder, with substantially more than a minimum hand, receives a Jump response, he should likewise consider the possibilities of a Slam; if he receives a weak, limiting response, he should generally dismiss this consideration; while if the response is of an Exploratory character, he should merely make the bid most likely to encourage Responder to show his full strength.

On his second bid, Responder may discourage the Slam, may continue exploration, or, not infrequently, invite the Slam himself.

In practically all Slam bidding, the first step is to *establish the suit* in which the hand should be played. The next step is the Slam Invitation which partakes of a dual nature, in that, first, it conveys the information to partner that we are interested in a Slam, and second, it requests information as to whether or not he is interested. The Slam Invitation consists of a bid of a new suit, a Jump to game

---

* The one exception to this is the final contract of four notrump. Although this is more than game, it is still two tricks below the Slam. Hence, there are many instances where a final contract of four notrump is proper.

when a lower bid would not be passed, or a bid beyond game.

If not interested, partner signs off by returning to the fitted suit if the Slam Invitation has been in another suit; otherwise by passing.

If interested, he may bid a new suit. This is control-showing and indicates either the Ace or a void. A control-showing bid, made above the game level, almost demands a Slam. If made below the game level, it may be of a mild Exploratory nature. A Slam Invitation may also be accepted by a player who cannot make a control-showing bid. In this instance, he bids beyond game in the fitted suit.

CHAPTER XXII

The Slam Invitation

IN THIS chapter we shall illustrate the various Slam Invitational bids, and the acceptances and refusals thereof.

THE BID OF A NEW SUIT

Case I.

Bidder	Responder
1 ♠	3 ♠
4 ♣	

Here the four-club bid constitutes the Slam Invitation. Suppose the hands are:

Bidder	Responder
♠ A K x x	♠ Q J x x x
♡ A Q J	♡ K x x
◇ x x	◇ A x
♣ A x x x	♣ Q 10 x (a sound though not particularly strong three-spade response.)

After the Slam Invitation, Responder bids four diamonds, a *Nominal Acceptance,* showing the Ace of diamonds but not taking the bidding beyond game. Bidder now makes a control-showing bid of four hearts, still keeping below the game level. Responder, who has shown his full strength, now bids four spades, placing the responsibility for further action on Bidder. Bidder should pass; he has shown the full strength of his hand, first, by the Slam Invitation of four clubs and second by the control-showing bid of four hearts.

Let us improve the Bidder's hand in playing strength without changing the high card value.

He holds

♠ A K x x   ♡ A Q J x   ◇ x   ♣ A x x x

With this hand, the bidding would proceed in exactly the same manner up to the point where Responder signs off with four spades. Now Bidder would refuse the Sign-off and bid five spades, practically commanding Responder to bid six, which Responder would, of course, do.

Returning to Bidder's original hand and changing Responder's to

♠ Q J x x x   ♡ K x x x   ◇ A   ♣ Q 10 x

the bidding would again proceed in the same manner up to the four-heart bid. Now Responder, with a sound three-spade bid, fitting cards in both hearts and clubs, and the singleton Ace of diamonds, should not content himself with a Sign-off at four spades. He should jump to five spades, whereupon Bidder would of course bid six.

Case 2.

Bidder	Responder
1 ♡	2 ♡
4 ◇ (The Slam Invitation)	

This is one of the instances where Bidder invites a Slam,

even though partner has merely given a single limiting Raise. His hand might be:

♠ x   ♡ A K x x x   ◇ A J x x x   ♣ A x

Should Responder hold

♠ A x x   ♡ Q x x   ◇ x x x   ♣ K x x x

High card value 6.

but no distributional support, Responder would merely sign off at four hearts.

Suppose Responder's hand were slightly stronger distributionally, such as:

♠ A x x   ♡ Q x x x   ◇ x x   ♣ K x x x

Now Responder, with a very sound Raise to two hearts, should bid four spades, a control-showing bid above the game level, and hence, like all bids above the game level, practically demanding a Slam bid. Bidder would accept by making a control-showing bid of five clubs. Responder would bid five hearts, and Bidder would contract for the Small Slam.

Case 3.

Bidder	Responder
1 ♠	2 ♡
3 ♡	4 ♣ (The Slam Invitation)

Responder holds

♠ Q x x   ♡ K Q 10 x x   ◇ x   ♣ A J 10 x

With a good heart suit, a fit for partner's spades, a singleton diamond, and the strong clubs, Responder must give a

Slam Invitation after Bidder shows the heart fit. Should Bidder hold

♠ A K x x   ♡ A J x x   ◇ Q x x   ♣ x x

he would sign off with four hearts, having no additional values.

With a slightly better hand, including the King of clubs instead of the Queen of diamonds, Bidder would jump to five hearts, denying the Ace of diamonds (by his failure to make the control bid of four diamonds), but practically demanding that Responder bid a Slam with but one loser in that suit.

THE JUMP TO GAME

Case 1.

Bidder	Responder
1 ♡	1 ♠
4 ♠ (The Slam Invitation)	

Bidder holds

♠ A Q x x   ♡ A Q x x x   ◇ x   ♣ A J x

On this bidding, Responder must realize that the important cards in his hand for Slam purposes must be high cards in spades or hearts, or a side Ace. Should he hold

♠ K J x x x   ♡ x x x   ◇ K x x   ♣ K x

he should pass four spades, as he is reasonably certain that one of his Kings will be of no help and that his three small hearts indicate a very probable loser in that suit.

Again, changing Responder's hand so that he holds the King of hearts, instead of one of the minor-suit Kings, he should bid five spades over four spades, again denying first-round control in clubs or diamonds. However, Bidder, with three Aces and a singleton, would not fear to contract for the Small Slam.

Case 2.

Bidder	Responder
1 ♡	1 ♠
4 ♡ (The Slam Invitation)	

Bidder holds

♠ J x   ♡ A K Q J x x x   ◊ A K x   ♣ x

Here Responder should read the Slam Invitation as indicating a solid heart suit and first- or second-round control of both side suits. This Slam Invitational bid definitely fixes hearts as the fitted suit. Under no circumstances should Responder bid four spades as a rescue bid. Therefore, a bid of four spades by Responder would be an acceptance of the Slam Invitation, and could not be made to show a hand such as

♠ K Q 10 9 x x x   ♡ —   ◊ x x x   ♣ x x x

With this hand, Responder must pass.

Suppose Responder holds

♠ A K Q x x   ♡ x x   ◊ x x x   ♣ x x x

Over the four heart bid, Responder should accept the Slam Invitation by a bid of four spades. Bidder would now make a control-showing bid of five diamonds, whereupon Responder would merely bid five hearts, and Bidder would then contract for the Slam.

Case 3.

Bidder	Responder
1 of a suit	3 N T

The three-notrump response indicates a balanced hand with a high card value of from 10½ to 12. Bidder must consider a further bid if he has additional values.

Case 4.

Bidder	Responder
1 ♠	2 ♦
2 N T	4 ♠

or

Bidder	Responder
1 ♠	2 ♦
2 ♠	4 ♠

In each of these instances, Responder's second-round Jump has been a Slam Invitation. The exact significance of these bids will be taken up in Part III in the chapter "The Four Aces Exploratory Response."

THE BID BEYOND GAME

Case 1.

Bidder	Responder
1 ♡	1 ♠
3 ♠	5 ♠ (A Positive Slam Invitation)

Responder holds

♠ K J 10 x x x   ♡ K x   ◇ K J x x   ♣ x

He is unable to make a control-showing bid, but with sec-

ond-round control in all suits, he is very anxious for a Slam
after Bidder's Qualified Force. Should Bidder hold

♠ AQxx   ♥ AQJxxx   ♦ x   ♣ Kx

a very sound three-spade bid, he would nevertheless pass,
since he would realize that there was a loser in each of the
minor suits.

With a hand such as the following:

♠ Qxxx   ♥ QJ10xx   ♦ AQ   ♣ AK

which is also a sound three-spade bid, he likewise should
pass, since he would reason that his great strength in diamonds and clubs would be in part duplication, and Responder might well hold neither the Ace of hearts nor
the Ace of spades.

Case 2.

Bidder	*Responder*
1 ♦	2 N T
4 N T	
or 5 N T	
or 6 N T	

The two-notrump response has indicated that Responder
holds a high card value of from 8½ to 10½ and a balanced hand.

A four-notrump (a Nominal Slam Invitation) by Bidder invites Responder to bid more, only if his two-notrump has been a maximum or near maximum.

A five-notrump bid (a Positive Slam Invitation) commands him to bid six, unless his two-notrump should be
shaded or the barest minimum, but under no circumstances
to bid seven.

A six-notrump bid guarantees six and invites seven.

Examples of Bidder's action following the two-notrump response:

♠ A Q x   ♡ Q x   ◇ A K J x   ♣ K x x x

High card value 12½.

Bid four notrump. Combined with a maximum two-no-trump (10½), the total high card value will be 23, and there should be better than an even play for six; combined with a weak two-notrump, there should be practically no play for six, but four must be safe.

♠ A Q x   ♡ Q x   ◇ A K J x   ♣ A x x x

High card value 13½.

Bid five notrump.

♠ A Q x   ♡ Q x   ◇ A K J x   ♣ A Q x x

High card value 14½.

Bid six notrump. Even though Responder has a minimum two-notrump, the combined high card value will be 23; while if he has a maximum two-notrump, we wish him to contract for seven.

CHAPTER XXIII

When to Give or Accept a Slam Invitation
(Including the Rule of the Ace and the King)

IN THE preceding chapter, we illustrated various Slam
Invitational bids, in order to show *how* to bid a Slam. In
this chapter we shall take up *when* to invite or bid a Slam.

The first consideration is, of course, the actual strength
of our hand, and unless we hold substantially more than
the minimum indicated by our initial bids, we have no excuse, either for inviting the Slam ourselves or for accepting
a mild invitation. With a hand that has substantially more
than this minimum, we next consider our partner's bids.

In many cases, the Slam Invitation may be given by a
simple application of the Theory of Limits, combined
with common sense. For instance, any time our partner
makes a Jump bid in notrump, we may consider Slam
possibilities by simply combining our high card value with
his and giving proper allowance to additional tricks which
may be developed if we have a long suit.

When we open the bidding and partner gives an immediate single Raise in our suit, we may also consider giving
the Slam Invitation. For example:

Bidder	Responder
1 ♡	2 ♡
4 ◇ (Slam Invitation)	

Here Bidder should have a very strong hand, close to an Opening Forcing bid, such as:

♠ A x   ♡ A Q x x x   ◊ A Q x x x   ♣ x

Let us now consider what Responder should do after Bidder has given him a single Raise. In order to make a Slam Invitation, Responder should use the following yardstick: *If Responder's hand, in itself, is a sound Opening bid, he should invite a Slam.*

For example:

Bidder	Responder
1 ♠	2 ♡
3 ♡	4 ♣ (Slam Invitation)

Responder holds

♠ x x x   ♡ A K x x x   ◊ J x   ♣ A Q x

High card value 9½.

A sound Opening bid.

THE RULE OF THE ACE AND THE KING

The most important single bid leading to a Slam is the Double Raise of your partner's suit. In considering the action of either Bidder or Responder after this Double Raise, the authors have originated the rule of the Ace and the King. This rule is the first method so far devised to decide which hands warrant a Slam Invitation. Other Slam bidding rules have been made merely for the purpose of telling you how to bid a Slam. This rule of the Four Aces System tells you when to bid or invite a Slam.

This simple but highly important rule is as follows: When your partner gives you a double Raise in your suit, you should invite a Slam—

(a) With a balanced hand, if you can remove an Ace from your hand and still have a sound bid or response, or

' (b) With an unbalanced hand—a hand with a singleton or a void—when you can remove a King from your hand and still have a sound bid or response.

We must consider this rule from two angles, (1) that of the Bidder, and (2) that of the Responder.

In considering the Bidder, our problem is quite simple, as our limits are clearly defined by that of the Opening bid of one of a suit. For example, consider the two hands given below.

(1) ♠ AKxxx   ♡ AJx   ◇ xx   ♣ Axx
(2) ♠ AKxxx   ♡ Axx   ◇ Kxxx   ♣ x

You bid one spade and your partner jumps to three spades. In the first example (a balanced hand), deduct your Ace of clubs and you still have an Opening bid. In the second (an unbalanced hand), you are able to deduct the King of diamonds. Hence either hand warrants a Nominal Slam Invitation.*

In considering the Responder, we must first take up what constitutes a normal One-Over-One response. In our chapter on Responses, we pointed out that a hand such as

♠ KJxxx   ♡ xxx   ◇ xx   ♣ xxx

High card value 2½.

is a proper One-Over-One response to partner's Opening bid. While this is a proper response, it is not normal.

In order that the reader may apply the Rule of the Ace

---

*With either of these hands, we are not strong enough for a further Slam Invitation unless partner makes a Positive Acceptance, since in the first instance, that of the balanced hand, we are just one Ace above a minimum bid, and in the second, that of the unbalanced hand, just one King.

and the King as Responder, we are giving the following examples of hands which are normal One-Over-One responses. In the case of the balanced examples, an additional Ace would warrant a Slam Invitation, in the event that Bidder jumped to three in Responder's suit; in the case of the unbalanced hands, an additional King.

♠ A J 10 x   ♡ K x x   ◇ x x x x   ♣ x x

High card value 5½.

♠ Q 10 x x x   ♡ K x x   ◇ Q J x   ♣ x x

High card value 4½.

♠ x x   ♡ J x x x x   ◇ A x x   ♣ K x x

High card value 5½.

♠ A K x x x   ♡ x x x x   ◇ x x x   ♣ x

High card value 5.

♠ A Q x x   ♡ x   ◇ Q J x x   ♣ x x x x

High card value 5½.

♠ x   ♡ A J 9 x x   ◇ Q x x x x   ♣ x x

High card value 4½.

The following hands illustrate how the Rule of the Ace and the King is applied to the Responding Hand.*

Bidding:

Bidder	Responder
1 ♡	1 ♠
3 ♠	4 ◇ (Slam Invitation)

* In considering Responder's action within the meaning of this rule, the hand is not considered unbalanced if the singleton or void is in partner's suit.

♠ K Q x x   ♡ K x x   ◇ A x x   ♣ x x x

(Warrants a Slam Invitation)

Balanced hand—deducting the Ace of diamonds, we have

♠ K Q x x   ♡ K x x   ◇ x x x   ♣ x x x

(A normal response)

Bidding:

Bidder	Responder
1 ♣	1 ♡
3 ♡	4 ♣ (Slam Invitation)

♠ x   ♡ K Q x x x   ◇ K x x x   ♣ K x x

(Warrants a Slam Invitation)

Unbalanced hand—deducting the King of clubs, we have

♠ x   ♡ K Q x x x   ◇ K x x x   ♣ x x x

(A normal response)

Bidding:

Bidder	Responder
1 ♣	1 ♠
3 ♠	4 ♡ (Slam Invitation)

♠ A Q J x x   ♡ A x x   ◇ x x x   ♣ x x

(Warrants Slam Invitation)

Balanced hand—deducting the Ace of hearts, we have

♠ A Q J x x   ♡ x x x   ◇ x x x   ♣ x x

(A normal response)

In considering the Slam Invitation, the reader must **bear** in mind that the word "invitation" means exactly what it says, i.e., you do not have to bid the Slam.

Having invited a Slam, your subsequent action should be based on the values you hold in excess of the minimum necessary to give the invitation.

WHEN TO ACCEPT SLAM INVITATIONS

There are two types of Acceptances of Slam Invitations, namely:

(1) The Nominal Acceptance
(2) The Positive Acceptance

The Nominal Acceptance, which is control-showing, is made only below the game level, and, although encouraging, does not mean that a Slam should be bid. This Nominal Acceptance is made when the previous bidding has been sound and you can conveniently make a control-showing bid below the game level.

The Positive Acceptance (one trick less than a Slam) practically demands a Slam. It permits partner to pass in two situations, i.e.,

(1) Where he has slightly overbid
(2) When he believes that the combined hands have not sufficient controls.

This Positive Acceptance is made when a player has previously not shown the full strength of his hand, and is certain of making the above game contract, in the rare event that the Slam is not bid.

In giving and accepting Slam Invitations, the matter of first- and second-round controls is of tremendous importance. Remember that you can only make a Slam if the combined hands have first-round control of three suits and second-round control of the fourth.

CHAPTER XXIV

The Slam Invitational Game Force

THE RESPONSE OF THREE IN A LOWER RANKING SUIT

SINCE any bid of a new suit is a Temporary Force, there is no need of crowding the bidding by a first-round Jump when game is Responder's only objective. Hence, we reserve the immediate Jump in a new suit as a Slam Invitation. This bid informs partner that game is certain and that our main consideration is whether or not we can make a Slam.

The actual high card strength necessary for this Slam Invitation varies greatly. With strong support for partner's suit plus a fine suit of your own, 8 or 8½ might justify such a bid. With no support for partner's suit and no good suit of your own, it is necessary that your hand have a high card value of more than 12.*

The full value of the above procedure will become apparent when we consider the significance of Responder's second bid. His first bid is a Slam Try. His second bid gives further information. If it is a Raise of partner's suit or a rebid of his own suit, it usually indicates the suit in which Responder wants the Slam. Even though it is a bid

---

* There is one pattern with which it is particularly undesirable to give a Slam Invitational Game Force, namely: with a singleton of your partner's suit and three four-card suits.

of game only, Bidder is expected to bid again with anything over a minimum. If it is a bid of a new suit, it indicates that Responder is still exploring. Finally, if it is a bid of three notrump, it conveys the message that the Slam Invitational Game Force was based on high cards in excess of the maximum for an immediate three-notrump response.

The following hands illustrate:

♠ A K x x   ♡ K Q J x x x   ◊ x x   ♣ x

High card value 8½.

Over partner's Opening one-spade, Responder should bid three hearts. This is a minimum three-heart bid— excellent support for *partner's suit* and a fine suit of his own justify the Slam Invitation. Responder's second bid must be a return to spades.

♠ A x   ♡ K J x x x   ◊ A x x   ♣ A x x

High card value 11½.

In response to partner's one-heart, bid three clubs. This hand has splendid trump support. It has no suit but its substantial high card holding more than compensates. With this very fine hand your second bid should be five hearts, practically commanding six. A bid of only four hearts would put too much strain on your partner.

♠ x   ♡ K x x   ◊ A K Q J x x x   ♣ A x

High card value 11½.

Bid three diamonds over one spade. With this hand, support for partner's suit is not necessary, since you have a solid suit of your own and a substantial high card holding. Following the answer to this Jump bid, you should bid six diamonds, strongly inviting seven. When a player contracts for a Slam in a suit which has not been supported by partner, he should be prepared to play it with a void in partner's hand.

♠ Q x x   ♡ A K x x x   ◇ A x x   ♣ K x

High card value 11.

Bid three hearts over one spade. This is an example of the hand which has fair trump support, a fair suit, and a goodly share of high cards. Should partner bid three no-trump, we pass.

CHAPTER XXV

Slam Bidding After an Opening
One-Notrump Bid

THE Limiting feature of the Opening one-notrump makes subsequent Slam bidding a fairly easy matter.

In the event that Responder's hand is also of a notrump pattern, his high card value will indicate whether he should invite a Slam by bidding four notrump, beg for a Slam by bidding five, invite seven by bidding six, or bid seven himself. These bids have been discussed under "Responses to the Opening One Notrump." The high card holdings necessary are:

> Four Notrump—High card value of 9½ to 10.
> Five Notrump—High card value of 10½ to 11.
> Six Notrump—High card value of 11½ to 12.

Should the Responder have a strong, unbalanced hand, he will force in his suit.

If the Force is made in a minor, it is always a Slam Invitation.* The Original Bidder, with either a good notrump or strong support for his partner's suit may take the bidding past the three-notrump level.

If the Force is made in a major, it may not be a Slam Invitation, but it does show a good hand. The Original

---

* Otherwise, Responder should raise the notrump.

206

Bidder should carry the bidding beyond game only with
the absolute maximum.

Specific examples are:

Bidder	High card value	Responder
♠ K x x x	2	♠ A Q J x x x
♡ K Q x	3	♡ J x x
◇ A K x	5	◇ x
♣ A 10 x	3	♣ K x x

13 with 7 honors.

Bidding:

Bidder	Responder
1 N T	3 ♠ [1]
4 ♣ [2]	4 ♠ [3]
5 ◇ [4]	6 ♠ [5]

[1] In this instance merely a Force to game.
[2] Control Showing—the Slam Invitation.
[3] A Sign-off.
[4] A second control-showing bid—denotes a maximum
notrump.
[5] Accepts the second invitation.

Bidder	High card value	Responder
♠ A Q x	4	♠ x x
♡ Q J x x	1½	♡ x x
◇ K x	2	◇ A Q J x x x
♣ K Q J x	3½	♣ A x x

11 with 8 honors.

Bidding:

Bidder	Responder
1 N T [1]	3 ◊ [2]
3 N T [3]	Pass

[1] A minimum.
[2] A Slam Invitation.
[3] A Sign-off.

Bidder	High card value	Responder
♠ A J x	3½	♠ K Q x x x x
♡ K J x	2½	♡ A Q x
◊ K Q x	3	◊ A x
♣ K J 10 x	2½	♣ x x

11½ with 9 honors.

Bidding:

Bidder	Responder
1 N T	3 ♠
3 N T [1]	4 ◊ [2]
4 ♠ [3]	5 ♡ [4]
5 N T [5]	6 N T [6]
Pass	

[1] A Sign-off.
[2] The Slam Invitation.
[3] A second Sign-off.
[4] The second Slam Invitation.
[5] Accepting the Slam Invitation in notrump.
[6] Contracting for the Slam which should be safe in notrump. If Responder had a singleton, he would have bid six spades.

CHAPTER XXVI

Slam Bidding in Competitive Situations

SLAM BIDDING WHEN THE OPPONENTS ENTER THE BIDDING

IN MANY instances, defensive bidding will warn you away from a Slam; in others, it will make it difficult for you to reach a Slam; but occasionally it will help you. For instance, consider the following hands:

Bidder	Responder
♠ K 10 x x x x	♠ —
♡ A x x x	♡ K Q x x x
◇ A Q x	◇ K J x x x
♣ —	♣ x x

With no adverse action, the bidding might well proceed: one spade, two hearts, four hearts, and while seven would be made, probably not even six would be bid. However, suppose that the one-spade were overcalled by a bid of two clubs. Responder would then make a Free bid of two hearts, whereupon the Original Bidder would be able to make a cue bid in clubs, and either six or seven hearts would be contracted for, depending on how well the bidding developed.

The preceding hand was given to show the value of cue bidding. When the opponents make no bid, a player must be careful that his control-showing bid will not be misread, but when an opponent does bid a suit, a player can always show control of that suit without risking misinterpretation by his partner.

Of course, there are frequent occasions when a control should not be shown. For instance, you open the bidding with one spade holding

♠ K Q x x x ♡ A x x ◇ — ♣ K Q J x x

High card value 9½.

and the bidding proceeds: two diamonds by Senior, two spades by Responder, and three diamonds by Junior. At this point you decide that six will almost surely be made against any but a heart opening. As a cue bid of diamonds would be a strong invitation to your opponents to lead some other suit, your best procedure is to make a control-showing bid of three hearts, in order to discourage a heart lead.

SLAM BIDDING BY THE DEFENDING SIDE *

There are two general instances when the Defending Side may successfully contract for a Slam; first, when the Opening bid has been a psychic; second, when, although the Opening bid has been sound, the presence of void suits and singletons render the Opening Bidder's high cards useless.

The following specific illustrations will show how such Slams are arrived at:

You are Junior and hold

♠ K x x x x ♡ — ◇ x ♣ A K x x x x

Bidding:

Bidder	Senior	Responder	Junior (You)
1 ♡	1 ♠	Pass	?

* The opponents of the Opening Bidder.

Bid six spades or, if you wish to invite seven, you may first cue bid in hearts, then bid clubs, and next jump to six spades.

You are Senior and hold

♠ A Q J x x   ♡ x   ♢ A Q J x x   ♣ K x

Bidding:

Bidder	Senior (You)	Responder	Junior
1 ♡	Double [1]	Pass	1 ♠
Pass	4 ♠ [2]	Pass	5 ♣ [3]
Pass	6 ♠ [4]	Pass	Pass
Pass			

[1] Not quite strong enough to make a Game Forcing Overcall in the opponents' suit.

[2] Even though Junior has a blank hand, you should have a good play for the contract.

[3] Slam Invitation—a control-showing bid.

[4] Junior would not have made the control-showing bid on the Ace of clubs alone, and hence you know he has other values. Therefore, you realize that at worst the Slam will depend upon a finesse, and the Opening bid indicates that the finesse will be right.

You are Senior and hold

♠ A Q x   ♡ K x   ♢ A 10 x x   ♣ A 10 x x

Bidding:

Bidder	Senior (You)	Responder	Junior
1 ♠	1 N T	Pass	3 ♢
Pass	?		

At this point you are certain that the Opening bid was either psychic or semi-psychic. Therefore, you decide to invite a Slam strongly, and make a control-showing bid of three spades. Should Junior sign off with with three notrump, you then jump to five diamonds, a second Slam Invitation.

CHAPTER XXVII

Slam Practice

IN THIS chapter we illustrate the theories of Slam bidding discussed in the previous chapters.

Bidder	Responder
♠ A x	♠ K J
♡ A Q x x x	♡ K J 10 x
◇ A Q x	◇ x x x
♣ x x x	♣ K Q x x

High card value 11.   High card value 8.

Bidding:

Bidder	Responder
1 ♡	3 ♡
3 ♠ [1]	4 ♡ [2]
Pass [3]	

[1] Bidder, with a balanced hand, can subtract an Ace and still have a bid. He invites a Slam after the double raise, in accordance with the Rule of the Ace and the King.

[2] Signing-off.

[3] No excess values.

213

Bidder	Responder
♠ K Q x x x x	♠ J 9 x x
♡ K Q x x	♡ A x
◊ x	◊ A K x x
♣ A x	♣ x x x

High card value 9.   High card value 8½.

Bidding:

Bidder	Responder
1 ♠	3 ♠
4 ♣ [1]	4 ◊ [2]
4 ♠ [3]	5 ♡ [4]
6 ♠ [5]	Pass

[1] Slam Invitation made in accordance with *the Rule of the Ace and the King* (Unbalanced hand—deduct a King).

[2] Nominal Acceptance, showing a control.

[3] The hand does not warrant a stronger bid.

[4] Positive Acceptance, showing another control.

[5] The Slam should be made.

Bidder	Responder
♠ A K Q 9 6 3 2	♠ 10 7 4
♡ 3	♡ A Q J 10 6 5
◊ K 8	◊ Q J 4
♣ A 10 7	♣ 3

High card value 11.   High card value 6.

Bidding:

Bidder	Responder
1 ♠	2 ♡ [1]
4 ♠ [2]	5 ♠ [3]
6 ♠ [4]	Pass

[1] An Exploratory response.
[2] A Slam Invitation—the unnecessary Jump to game.
[3] Positive acceptance beyond game, but denies control of either clubs or diamonds.
[4] Bids the Slam.

Bidder	Responder
♠ A K J x x	♠ Q 10 9 x
♡ x	♡ A Q x x
◊ A Q J 9 x	◊ 10 x
♣ K x	♣ J x x

High card value 12.   High card value 5½.

Bidding:

Bidder	Responder
1 ♠	2 ♠
4 ◊ [1]	4 ♡ [2]
6 ♠ [3]	Pass

[1] A Slam Invitation, indicating a hand almost as strong as an original Forcing bid.
[2] Nominal Acceptance, showing a control and a sound Raise.
[3] At the worst the Slam should depend on a finesse, which is the case here. Responder would have bid the same if he held the King of diamonds instead of the Queen of hearts and Jack of clubs.

Bidder	Responder
♠ x	♠ A x x
♡ A x x x	♡ K J 10 x x
◇ K Q J x x	◇ x x
♣ K x x	♣ A x x

High card value 8½. High card value 8½.

Bidding:

Bidder	Responder
1 ◇	1 ♡
2 ♡	2 ♠ [1]
3 ♡ [2]	4 ♣ [3]
5 ♡ [4]	6 ♡
Pass	

[1] Slam Invitation—Responder has a sound original bid.

[2] Sign-off.

[3] Second control-showing bid.

[4] Acceptance of the Slam Invitation above the game level.

The Slam Invitation need not be control-showing. However, when the Slam Invitation is followed by a cue bid in another suit by the same bidder, it means that the Slam Invitation was also control-showing.

Bidder signs-off the first time, as he does not care to encourage a Slam with his slightly more than minimum holding. After the second control-showing bid, his hand in combination with his partner's appears much stronger, and he makes a Positive Acceptance of Responder's Slam Invitation.

Bidder	Responder
♠ A	♠ K J x
♥ K Q J x x x	♥ A 10 x
♦ A x x	♦ K Q x x
♣ K x x	♣ Q x x

High card value 11½. High card value 9½.

Bidding:

Bidder	Responder
1 ♥	2 N T
3 ♥ [1]	4 ♥ [2]
4 ♠ [3]	5 ♥ [4]
6 ♥ [5]	Pass

[1] Responder cannot pass. Bidder desires further information in order to decide whether to bid six or seven.

[2] Support for Bidder's suit.

[3] A control-showing bid above the game level.

[4] The Sign-off.

[5] Bidder knows that Responder either does not hold the Ace of clubs or feels that he is too weak to show it.

Bidder	Responder
♠ A K x x	♠ Q x
♥ K x x x	♥ A Q x
♦ A 10	♦ K J x x
♣ Q 10 x	♣ A J x x

High card value 11.   High card value 11.

Bidding:

Bidder	Responder
1 ♠	3 N T [1]
5 N T [2]	6 N T [3]
Pass	

[1] Sound—11 with eight honors.
[2] Almost demands six.
[3] Bids the Slam. Although the combined high card value is but 22, the play for a Slam is very good, due to the great number of honors held.

Bidder	Responder
♠ A K J x	♠ Q 10 x
♡ J x	♡ A x x x
◇ K J x x	◇ A Q x
♣ A Q x	♣ K x x

High card value 12½.   High card value 10.

Bidding:

Bidder	Responder
1 ♠	2 N T
4 N T [1]	6 N T
Pass	

[1] Slam Invitation above the game level. Requests partner to bid the Slam if his holding is close to a maximum two-notrump.

The Opening Bidder has a high card value of 12½, which in combination with a maximum two-notrump (10 or 10½) should produce a Slam. (A point count of 22½, even without a five-card or longer suit, will produce a Slam more than fifty percent of the time.)

Bidder	*Responder*
♠ K Q x	♠ A 109 x x x
♡ A Q J x x x	♡ K x
◇ A x	◇ x x x
♣ x x	♣ A x

High card value 10½.   High card value 8.

Bidding:

Bidder	*Responder*
1 ♡	1 ♠
3 ♡ ¹	3 ♠
4 ♠ ²	5 ♣ ³
5 ◇ ⁴	5 ♡ ⁵
7 ♠ ⁶	Pass

¹ A Qualified Game Force.
² Showing spade support in addition to a strong heart suit. Can be read as a Slam Invitation.
³ A Positive Acceptance—a control-showing bid beyond game.
⁴ More than willing to show the Ace of diamonds.
⁵ All the other controls having been shown, Responder shows the King of partner's suit, inviting a Grand Slam.*
⁶ Seven must be made with solid hearts and spades and control of all four suits.

* It is a common-sense rule that when one player shows a control and his partner subsequently raises the control suit, he is showing the King. This secondary control-showing bid is only used when it is intended as a Positive Slam Acceptance. In the hand given above, spades have become the fitted suit—Responder's delayed heart bid must be control-showing.

CHAPTER XXVIII

The Two-Bid

In PART I of the book we briefly discussed the requirements for an Opening two-bid, i.e.,

(A) A hand with a high card holding of at least 13, which might occasionally be reduced to 11 with freakish hands.

(B) A probable playing strength of within one trick of game.*

While the primary purpose of the two-bid lies in getting to game, it has a very important secondary purpose—getting to a Slam. When we bid two originally, we expect our partner to investigate Slam possibilities thoroughly and to bid one with very few high cards. An original two-bid with a hand such as the following:

♠ A K Q J 10 x x x x x   ♡ x   ◇ x   ♣ x

would defeat this purpose, as Responder with the Ace-King of a side suit and Kings of both of the others, would immediately visualize seven, whereas we could not make six. Furthermore, in the event that your partner's holding should be so weak that he would pass your one-spade bid,

---

* A high card value of 18½ or more automatically qualifies a hand as an Opening two-bid, regardless of playing strength.

your opponents would have most of the high cards, and you would find yourself defending.

While it is a simple matter to arrive at the high card strength of a hand, the determination of the playing strength requires study. In computing the trick-taking ability of long suits, the player should arbitrarily assume neutral support in partner's hand.* This neutral support is arrived at by placing approximately one-third of the remaining cards of the suit in partner's hand. Thus, if you have a six-card suit, partner should normally hold two of the suit, while with a five-card, he should hold three. In the event that your five- or six-card suit should be headed by the two top honors, there should normally be one loser; if headed by the three top honors, there should normally be no losers.

Examples of two-bids are:

♠ A K x x x (4**)   ♡ A K Q (3)   ◇ K Q J (2)   ♣ A x (1)

Playing tricks 10; High card value 17½; Bid 2 ♠

♠ A K x x x x (5)   ♡ A K Q x x (5)   ◇ x   ♣ x

Playing tricks 10; High card value 11; Bid 2 ♠

♠ K Q J (2)   ♡ A Q J 10 x (4)   ◇ —   ♣ A K x x x (4)

Playing tricks 10; High card value 13; Bid 2 ♡

♠ A K J 10 x x (5½)   ♡ K Q J 10 (3)   ◇ A x x (1)   ♣ —

Playing tricks 9½; High card value 12; Bid 2 ♠

♠ A K x (2)   ♡ A Q J (2)   ◇ A K x (2)   ♣ A K x x (2½)

Playing tricks 8½; High card value 19½; Bid 2 ♣

---

* Subsequent bidding may of course change this impression of neutral support.

** Figures in parentheses represent playing-trick strength of each suit.

♠ x   ♡ x   ◇ A K Q J x x (6)   ♣ A K x x x (4)

Playing tricks 10; High card value 11½; Bid 2 ◇

RESPONSES TO THE TWO-BID

When we first played Contract, we used the two-bid as a very strong invitation to partner to respond. Finally, Mr. Waldemar von Zedtwitz suggested making the two-bid absolutely forcing and with an artificial two-notrump response to indicate a blank or near blank hand. This suggestion was immediately adopted by us, and others, many months before it was incorporated in any system of Bridge. Our original concept was, and is, that the artificial two-notrump response should be made only when no proper constructive bid may be found. With this concept in mind we are prepared to present our responses to the Opening two-bid.

*1. The Two-Notrump Response.** May conceivably include a high card value of 3½ but no more. It *denies* the strength for any other response.

*2. The Jump to Four of Partner's Suit.** Indicates a hand which due to its distributional features would be strong enough to raise a one-bid to two, but which contains no Ace or King. This new bid has been thoroughly tested over many months of play and found entirely satisfactory.

3. The Single Raise of Partner's Suit. Does not limit the strength of Responding Hand in any manner, since the Opening Bidder must continue. Under some circumstances, it may be made with as weak a trump holding as three small.

---

* The two-notrump response may be made with a hand which includes an Ace or King. The Jump to four of partner's suit absolutely denies an Ace or King. *Any response other than these two promises at least one Ace or King.*

4. The Response of Two of a Higher Ranking Suit.
This bid indicates a hand including an Ace or King with
which we would make a normal One-Over-One response to
partner's Opening one-bid.

5. The Response of Three of a Lower Ranking Suit.
As this bid brings the contract to the three-level, it must
be constructive. It may indicate a high card value of as low
as 3½ with a good five-card suit.

6. The Three-Notrump Response. This bid indicates a
value of 4 to 6 with little support for partner's suit, and
no suit of our own. With a greater high card value, bid
four notrump or another suit.

Examples of responses to Opening two-bids are

♠ Q x x x   ♡ Q x x x   ◇ x x   ♣ Q x x

High card value 3.

We respond with two-notrump to an Opening bid of two
clubs or two diamonds, but jump partner's bid of two
spades or two hearts to four, since our hand contains fine
trump support. Furthermore, due to the fact that this bid
denies a holding of any Ace or King, our partner will
not attempt a Slam with two losing tricks in any suit.
However, should his hand be something like

♠ A K J 10 x x   ♡ A   ◇ K Q   ♣ A K x x

he could clearly afford to bid a Slam.

♠ x x x   ♡ x x x   ◇ x x x   ♣ K J x x

High card value 2½.

Bid three clubs over an Opening two-club bid and two
notrump over any other two-bid.

♠ K Q J x   ♡ x x   ◇ x x x x   ♣ x x x

High card value 3½.

Bid two spades over an Opening bid of two in any suit, intending to sign-off thereafter.

♠ x x   ♡ K x x   ◇ K x x x   ♣ Q x x x

High card value 5.

Over an Opening bid of two spades, this hand calls for a three-notrump response, as we can neither raise spades nor bid a satisfactory suit of our own. We give an immediate single Raise if partner's Opening two-bid is in any other suit.

♠ J x   ♡ A x x   ◇ K x x x   ♣ Q x x x

High card value 6½.

This hand is so strong that we intend to bid a Slam. Should partner open with two hearts, diamonds, or clubs, we give an immediate single Raise as the first step. Over a two-spade bid, however, we can neither raise his suit nor bid a suit of our own and are too strong for a mere three-notrump response. Therefore, we bid four notrump.

DEVELOPMENT OF THE BIDDING AFTER A TWO-BID

The main point to bear in mind here is that since our two-bid has already indicated a tremendous hand we have no right to rebid our own values indefinitely, and furthermore, we must realize that certain responses, even though of a strength-showing nature, should not encourage us. For instance, consider the following hand:

♠ A K Q J 10 9 8   ♡ A K Q   ◇ A   ♣ x x

High card value 15½.

with eleven sure playing tricks, but where our only chance of taking tricks in partner's hand lies in clubs. Suppose partner's response to our Opening two-spade bid is three diamonds. We rebid to three spades and he bids four diamonds. Now even though five spades is absolutely certain, we cannot afford to bid more than four, since should we bid five, partner, with a holding such as

♠ x x   ♡ x x   ♢ K Q J 10 x x   ♣ Q J x

would be entitled to bid six. On the other hand, should we hold Ace-small of diamonds and a singleton club, we would bid six spades.

Again we bid two spades holding

♠ A K Q J x   ♡ A K Q x x   ♢ x x   ♣ x

High card value 12½.

and partner raises to three spades. At this point we must sign-off with four spades. Now if partner invites a Slam by a further bid, we encourage him by showing our hearts.

Another example:

♠ —   ♡ A K Q J 10 x x   ♢ A x x   ♣ A x x

High card value 12½.

Should partner respond to our Opening two hearts with two spades, we bid three hearts. If he now bids three no-trump we pass, as three notrump is absolutely certain and we cannot be sure that we will deliver four hearts. Should partner's response to our two hearts be three diamonds, we would also bid three hearts on the second bid. Now, even though he bid three notrump, we would nevertheless contract for six hearts, having first invited seven by a bid of four clubs.

CHAPTER XXIX

Responses to Two- and Three-Notrump Bids

RESPONSES TO THE OPENING TWO-NOTRUMP

THE Opening two-notrump bid shows a hand with a high card value of $14\frac{1}{2}$ to 16, every suit stopped, and no singleton. In responding, our problem is to act on the information given. The various responses at our disposal are

1. The Pass. Made with a hand containing high card strength of less than one King, or one Queen and a Jack.*

2. The Three-Notrump Response. (High card value of $1\frac{1}{2}$ to 6.) This response simply says: "Partner, as you want to play this hand at three notrump, there you are."

3. The Four-Notrump Response. (High card value of $6\frac{1}{2}$ to 7.) This bid says: "Partner, I know the maximum and minimum strength that your two-notrump bid shows. If you have close to a maximum two-notrump bid, let's bid a Slam; otherwise pass."

4. The Five-Notrump Response. (High card value of $7\frac{1}{2}$ to 8.) This bid says: "Partner, unless you have the veriest minimum two-notrump bid, I want to play this hand at six notrump. I am bidding five notrump merely to give you this option and also to tell you that I am not interested in seven."

* With a six-card major or a seven-card minor suit, respond without any high cards.

226

5. The Six-Notrump Response. (High card value of 8½ to 9.) This bid says: "Partner, even though you have a shaded bid, we cannot afford to play this hand short of a Slam, and if you have a strong two-notrump bid I am perfectly willing to have you bid seven."

Naturally, an immediate response of three, four, five or six notrump indicates a balanced hand; otherwise we would choose a suit response.

6. The Response of Three of a Suit. The Opening two-notrump Bidder has promised that if we respond he will carry on until a game bid is reached. Therefore, we may respond with three of a suit with any one of three hands:

First, a weak hand, but one with which we desire to give our partner the option of contracting for three notrump or game in our suit.

Second, a weak hand containing either a six-card major or seven-card minor suit that we intend to bid and rebid in minimums.

Third, a strong hand with which we intend subsequently to invite or bid a Slam.

7. The Jump to Four of a Suit. This is a specialized bid and says: "Partner, I intend to play the hand in this suit. If you have a maximum two-notrump we may make a Slam. You must decide."

Examples of responses to Opening two-notrump bids are as follows:

♠ x x   ♡ Q x x   ◇ Q x x x x   ♣ x x x

High card value 2.

Bid three notrump. You have two Queens.

♠ K x   ♡ x x x x   ◇ K x x x   ♣ Q x x

High card value 5.

Bid three notrump. The hand is not strong enough to invite a Slam.

♠ K x x   ♡ K x x   ◇ K x x x   ♣ Q x x

High card value 7.

Bid four notrump. If partner has a minimum two-notrump bid, we are still safe at four, while should he hold a maximum or near maximum, our combined hands have a value of 22½ or 23, which clearly indicates that a Slam will be made.

♠ K x x x   ♡ K x x   ◇ K x x   ♣ Q J x

High card value 7½.

Bid five notrump. We wish to play this hand at six.

♠ A x x   ♡ K x x   ◇ K J x x   ♣ Q J x

High card value 9.

Bid six notrump. Our high card value of 9, combined with the minimum of 14½ shown by the two-notrump bid, totals 23½. Should partner hold a 16-point hand, we have 25, which indicates a probable Grand Slam. Hence, we are well prepared for seven.

♠ K J x x x   ♡ x x   ◇ x x x   ♣ x x x

High card value 2½.

Bid three spades, intending to pass if partner bids three notrump or four spades.

♠ x x   ♡ x x x   ◇ K J x x x   ♣ x x x

High card value 2½.

Bid three notrump. There is no point in bidding three

diamonds as we do not want to play the hand at five diamonds.

♠ x x   ♡ x x x   ◇ Q J x x x x   ♣ x

High card value 1½.

Bid three diamonds. With this particular hand we intend to rebid our diamonds in minimums.

♠ x x   ♡ K Q J x x   ◇ A x x   ♣ x x x

High card value 6½.

Bid three hearts, intending to bid five hearts on the next round.

♠ K Q x x x x   ♡ x x   ◇ x x x   ♣ x x

High card value 3.

Bid three spades, intending to bid four spades over three notrump.

♠ K Q x x x x   ♡ x x   ◇ Q J x   ♣ x x

High card value 4½.

Bid four spades. We are now through bidding, as we have shown the full strength of our hand. If Bidder thinks that a Slam can be made, he should bid it.

♠ K Q x x x x   ♡ x x   ◇ K J x   ♣ x x

High card value 5½.

This hand is the same as the preceding one except for the substitution of the King for the Queen of diamonds. The additional value makes it imperative that we take stronger action. Accordingly, we bid three spades, intending subsequently to bid five spades.

♠ x x x x x x   ♡ x   ◇ x x x x x   ♣ x

High card value 0.

Bid three spades, intending to rebid the suit in minimums thereafter.

RESPONSES TO THE OPENING THREE-NOTRUMP

The Opening three-notrump bid has a high card value of 16½ to 18. We do not rescue an Opening three-notrump bid, hence, any response is constructive and suggests a Slam.

The various responses at our disposal are:

1. The Pass. Made with a hand with a high card value of less than 4½ and no workable suit.

2. The Four-Notrump Response. (High card value 4½ to 5.) This bid says: "Partner, if you have a near-maximum three-notrump we should bid a Slam."

3. The Five-Notrump Response. (High card value 5½ to 6.) This bid says: "Partner, unless you have shaded your three notrump, let us bid six, but not seven."

4. The Six-Notrump Response. (High card value 6½ to 7.) This bid says: "Partner, I guarantee six. Do you want to bid seven?"

5. The Bid of Four of a Suit. This bid says: "Partner, I have a workable suit which you may wish to raise."

6. The Bid of Five of a Suit. This bid practically commands six.

The following are examples of responses to Opening three-notrump bids:

♠ K x x   ♡ K x x x   ◇ x x x   ♣ Q x x

High card value 5.

Bid four notrump, obviously a safe contract. Partner may continue if his hand indicates a Slam.

♠ K x x   ♥ x x x   ♦ x x x x   ♣ Q x x

High card value 3.

Pass. Six is very improbable and even though four should be safe, there is danger in inviting partner to go further.

♠ K x x x   ♥ K x x x   ♦ Q x x   ♣ Q x

High card value 6.

Bid five notrump. We intend to play this hand at six.

♠ x x   ♥ K x x x x x   ♦ x x   ♣ x x x

High card value 2.

Bid four hearts. Our six-card heart suit may yield enough playing-tricks for a Slam.

Part III

CHAPTER XXX

Partial Scores

PARTIAL scores constitute a necessary complication in the game of Contract Bridge. There are eight possible scores for either side, each of which requires some modification of general bidding tactics. In view of its importance it is remarkable that many of the ablest partnerships known to the game do not seem to have the patience or willingness thoroughly to analyze the subject, in an effort to agree on the proper procedure when their side has a partial score. In this chapter we intend to outline certain general principles and to give some examples to illustrate how we modify our normal bidding in this situation.

First, let us consider partial scores of 20 and 30. With such a score, after the bidding has been opened by his side, the average player exhibits a marked tendency to continue to game automatically. The reason is quite apparent—the one trick less to contract for acts as a lure. When this tendency is unchecked players will find such a partial score to be a handicap rather than an advantage. They will frequently be severely penalized at a contract that will produce game with the aid of a partial score, whereas they would have otherwise stopped at the comparatively safe contract of one notrump or two of a suit. It does not pay to stretch a hand unduly merely because you need one trick less than usual to score game.

Second, partial scores of 40 and 60. As these not only occur most frequently but are also the most desirable, it is important to make the most of them. In order that they may be employed to the greatest advantage it is essential to make several important modifications in your general bidding tactics.

The first concerns the Opening one notrump. We do not modify the lower limit for this bid, but do increase the upper limit to include hands which are just too weak for a two-notrump bid. Hence, with a partial score of 40, we expect our partner to take out in his best four-card suit, even though his hand may be almost a blank.

While with a partial score of 40 or 60 there is practically no chance that partner will pass our opening one-bid, yet with many hands, if we do not open with two, the only way we can show our full strength is by jumping past game on a subsequent round, which might jeopardize the contract. In order to guard against this undesirable necessity we reduce the playing strength requirements of our two-bid to eight tricks.

The following hands are proper two-bids with a score of 40 or 60:

♠ A K Q J x x   ♡ A x x   ◊ A x x   ♣ x

High card value 12½.

♠ A x x   ♡ K Q J x x x   ◊ A x   ♣ A x

High card value 12½.

But the following hand should definitely be bid as one club only:

♠ A K x x   ♡ A K x x   ◊ x   ♣ A K x x

High card value 15.

With a bust the proper response to such an opening two-bid (except when the bid does not complete a game score) is a pass—the two-notrump response shows some slight high card strength, at least a King or two Queens.

While our opening suit bid with a partial score of 40 or 60 is not modified, our responses are. In the first place, we favor giving a Chance with practically anything, and such a hand as

♠ x x   ♡ Q x x   ◇ J x x x   ♣ 10 x x x

High card value 1½.

becomes a proper one-notrump response to an opening spade or heart bid, or a single Raise for an Opening club or diamond. This modification is purely a matter of common sense.

In the second place, when we consider that Exploratory responses of two are now bids of game and may be passed, we must realize that there is need for further modification of our responses. With 40 on score, we remove the limiting feature from the one-notrump response and deem it to be both Forcing and Exploratory, and, in fact, place it in the same category as the One-Over-One. With a big hand, we may respond to our partner's Opening suit bid with one notrump, intending to show our strength after his first forced rebid. With a weak hand we also bid one notrump, intending to pass thereafter.

Thirdly, Jump responses in notrump become slightly stronger than with no score and are always Slam Invitations. The same rule also applies to Jump Raises in a suit.

With partial scores of 70 to 90, Opening bids are the same as with 60 but responses become even more cramped because practically all bids are sufficient for game. The only way Responder can give a direct Slam try is either by a

Raise in partner's suit beyond game, a Jump in notrump, or a Jump in another suit.

The one-notrump response (if the Opening bid is sufficient for game) is encouraging. It does not indicate weakness and gives Bidder a chance to make a Slam Try, if he holds a maximum one-bid. Jump responses of two and three notrump are the same as with 60, and a single Raise in partner's suit, above game, is a mild Slam Invitation and indicates a hand which would probably warrant a Jump Raise were there no score. Higher Raises of partner's suit indicate correspondingly stronger hands.

Examples of how we bid hands with partial scores:

Partial score of 40.

	Bidder	Responder
♠	A K x x x x	♠ Q x x
♡	A x x	♡ K x x x
◇	K x	◇ A x x
♣	K x	♣ A x x

High card value 12.   High card value 9.

Bidding:

	Bidder	Responder
1	♠	1 N T [1]
2	♠ [2]	3 ♠ [3]
4	♡ [4]	5 ♣ [5]
6	♠ [6]	Pass [7]

[1] Intending to make some mild Slam Try on the next bid.
[2] The hand does not warrant a stronger bid at this point.

³ A Slam Invitation in spades based on the knowledge that the Bidder holds at least a five-card suit.

⁴ A control-showing bid.

⁵ Continuing the control-showing.

⁶ With the Kings of both diamonds and clubs our bid is perfectly sound.

⁷ Although Responder realizes that he and his partner have all the controls, nevertheless, there is no body to his own hand, and he has no short suits.

Partial score of 60.

Bidder	Responder
♠ A K Q J x x	♠ x x x x
♡ A x x	♡ K x x
◇ A x x	◇ K Q J x
♣ x	♣ x x

High card value 12½. High card value 5½.

Bidding:

Bidder	Responder
2 ♠	3 ♠
4 ◇ ¹	5 ◇ ²
5 ♡ ³	6 ♡ ⁴
6 ♠	Pass

¹ A control.

² Showing secondary control in diamonds.

³ A further control-showing bid.

⁴ Showing secondary control in hearts.

Partial score of 70.

Bidder	Responder
♠ A K x x x	♠ Q J x x
♡ A K x x	♡ x
◇ x x	◇ A K x x
♣ x x	♣ x x x x

High card value 10.   High card value 6½.

Bidding:

Bidder	Responder
1 ♠	2 ♠ [1]
Pass [2]	

[1] A mild Slam Try, as it is a Raise beyond game.
[2] The original Bidder realizes that by the Principle of Limits partner's bid of two spades clearly denies a hand which will produce a Slam.

Partial score of 40.

Bidder	Responder
♠ A Q x x	♠ J x
♡ A x x	♡ J 10 x x
◇ A Q x	◇ J x x x
♣ K Q x	♣ K x x

High card value 14.   High card value 3½.

Bidding:

Bidder	Responder
1 N T [1]	2 ♡ [2]
Pass	

[1] A super-strong one-notrump asking partner to show a four-card suit.

[2] Bidding his strongest four-card suit. With no score this hand would, of course, call for a pass by Responder.

Partial score of 40.

Bidder	Responder
♠ A K x x x	♠ x x
♡ A K x x x	♡ x x x x
◇ K x x	◇ Q x x
♣ —	♣ J x x x

High card value 12.   High card value 1½.

Bidding:

Bidder	Responder
1 ♠ [1]	1 N T [2]
3 ♡ [3]	Pass [4]

[1] This hand is not quite strong enough for a two-bid.
[2] With no score we should pass, but with 40 we make the one-notrump response, hoping that partner may bid a second suit.
[3] A definite Slam Invitation but not forcing.
[4] Nothing to ponder over here.

These combined hands fit perfectly and might actually produce a Slam, if spades and hearts break evenly.

COMPETITIVE BIDDING WITH PARTIAL SCORES

Possession of a partial score by either side results in a natural modification of our bidding tactics. If our opponents have 60 on score, we must anticipate that unless we defend they will score a game. Therefore, we somewhat weaken the requirements necessary for an overcall. We must at times take risks in an effort to push the opponents to an unmakable contract.

Illustrations:

♠ K x   ♥ A x x   ♦ A Q x x x   ♣ x x x

High card value 9.

Opening bid is one spade. With no score we would pass this hand, but if either side has a partial score, we take action. In this case, the action should not take the form of a two-diamond overcall. We would double informatorily, as we have fair preparation for a response in either clubs or hearts.

♠ Q J x x   ♥ A x x   ♦ A x x   ♣ A x x

High card value 10½.

Opening bid is one spade. With no score for either side we would make a trap pass, hoping that our opponents would get beyond their depth. When either side has a partial score, however, we would bid one notrump.

When the opponents have a partial score it may frequently be found desirable to open the bidding in first or second position with a slightly shaded hand for fear that if you pass you will be unable to get into action. For instance, you are Dealer, your opponents have a partial score of 60, and you hold:

♠ A x x   ♥ K x x   ♦ Q x x   ♣ A x x x

High card value 9.

If you pass originally and one of your opponents opens the bidding, it would then be dangerous indeed for you to take any action even though not vulnerable. However, an Opening one-club bid is not fraught with any particular danger and should be made primarily as an advance defensive measure.

SUMMARY OF PARTIAL SCORES

Partial scores are a necessary evil in Contract, and if you do not modify your bidding to allow for their effect you will find it not only almost impossible to bid Slams with any degree of accuracy but frequently will find yourselves either taking large penalties or being bluffed.

In the case of a score of 20 or 30, you should bid normally.

With 40 or 60 on score, the upper limit of strength for the opening one notrump is increased, and we may occasionally make such a bid with a High Card Value of as much as 15. With 40 on score, it is of course a very strong request to partner to select a suit.

With a partial score of 40 the change in the one-notrump response is very substantial. Instead of being limiting it becomes exploratory and of the same nature as the One-Over-One. If made with a weak hand, Responder will show this by passing on the second round; if made with a strong hand, he will show it by taking appropriate action on the second round.

With partial scores of 70 to 90 most players have a pronounced tendency to pass their partner's opening bid. Whenever your high card holding is more than 5, you should endeavor to make some bid, since otherwise you may be missing an easy Slam.

Defensive and competitive bidding with a partial score present many interesting problems.

When there is no score and you hold a strong but balanced hand, it is best to lie in wait, anticipating that you have no game yourself. If your opponents bid game you have a good chance to defeat them and thereby reap a profit; while if they stop short of game, the loss incurred will be slight. When they have a partial score, however, you should endeavor to enter the bidding, if only for the purpose of pushing them one trick beyond their depth; while if you have a partial score, you should bid in order to feel out the possibility of scoring game.

When your opponents have a partial score and you have a balanced hand in the borderline zone which ordinarily should be passed, it will frequently be found advisable to open the bidding. Should you pass, defensive action at a later stage of the bidding might be fraught with great danger.

CHAPTER XXXI

The Four Aces Exploratory Response

TWO OF A LOWER RANKING SUIT

THIS response is one of the most valuable bids in our system, as it enables both Responder and Bidder to explore game and Slam possibilities at a low range in the bidding.

Like the One-Over-One, it cannot be passed. Unlike the One-Over-One, which may be a very weak Chance-giving response, it must be a strength-showing bid. The reason is self-evident; you are one trick higher.

The following hand will illustrate this difference:

♠ xx   ♡ K 10x   ◇ Kxxxx   ♣ xxx

High card value 4.

Should partner's Opening bid be one club, our response is one diamond—a One-Over-One. Should his Opening bid be one spade, we would not be strong enough to take the bidding to the level of two, and would merely respond with one notrump.

The Exploratory response imparts such flexibility to our system that we have no need either to overbid or underbid. It is particularly useful on those hands which are too strong for one response and too weak for another. Furthermore, since it is a Temporary Force, it does away with doubtful first-round Jumps that crowd the bidding, and enables us to reserve the immediate Jump response in a new suit as a Slam Invitational Game Force.

This response is used:

First, when it is the logical and only bid.

Second, as a compromise between the various notrump responses.

Third, to avoid a difficult choice between a single or Jump Raise in partner's suit.

Fourth, with a hand which would also warrant a Jump bid in notrump or a Jump Raise in partner's suit, but where we prefer to explore in accordance with the Development or Flow Principle, rather than leap toward an arbitrary final contract.

Fifth, in preference to an unsafe two-notrump bid.

The following hands illustrate this response, the Opening bid in each instance being one spade:

Type 1.

♠ x x   ♡ x x   ◇ A K x x x x   ♣ x x x

High card value 5.

This is an obvious two-diamond bid; there is no other choice. Should partner merely rebid his spades to two, we pass; while if he bids two notrump, we raise to three no-trump.

Type 2.

♠ Q x   ♡ Q x x x   ◇ K Q x x   ♣ K J x

High card value 7½.

This hand, with a high card value of 7½ with 6 honors, is entirely too strong for a one-notrump response, but at the same time is not quite strong enough for a Game-Forcing response of two notrump. A two-diamond response enables us to make a bid of two notrump on the second round (highly invitational, but not Forcing), in the event that partner rebids to two spades.

Type 3.

(A)   ♠ K J x x   ♡ J x x   ◇ A Q x x   ♣ x x

High card value 7.

(B)   ♠ K x x   ♡ J x x   ◇ A Q x x x   ♣ x x

High card value 6½.

Hand A is almost a three-spade bid; Hand B is just too strong for a two-spade bid. With either hand, we respond with two diamonds. If partner's second bid is two spades, we bid three spades, urging him to bid game. In this instance, the Original Bidder may now pass if he has a bare minimum.

If partner's second bid is two notrump, with Hand A we bid three spades. This bid gives the Original Bidder the option of bidding either three notrump or four spades. The two-notrump bid has shown that the original bid was *not* a minimum—he cannot pass. With Hand B we bid three notrump, which should be easier to make than four spades.

If partner's second bid is two hearts, with Hand A we jump to three spades—a Game Force. With Hand B we merely bid two spades,* as we are not anxious to contract for game unless partner can find a further bid.

If partner's second bid is three clubs, our choice lies between three and four spades. The three-club bid is a

---

* The Return after an Exploratory response of two is not a Sign-off.

Skip Level Shift and shows that the Opening bid is not only more than a minimum, but may be a very strong hand of the two-suiter type. With Hand A we jump to four spades, a mild Slam Invitation—our splendid trump support justifies this bid. With Hand B we bid three spades, a constructive bid which will not be passed.

It is worthy of note that the weaker action taken with Hand B is due to the fact that it only includes three trumps in support of partner's spade bid.

Type 4.

♠ J x   ♡ A x x   ◇ A Q x x x   ♣ K x x

High card value 9½.

This hand fulfills all the requirements for a two-notrump response. However, if we respond with two notrump and partner bids either three spades or three notrump, we would have no chance to show our diamonds. While game would be safe, we might easily miss a Slam. Therefore, we respond with two diamonds.

Let us suppose that Bidder's hand was

♠ A 10 x x x   ♡ x   ◇ K x x x   ♣ A Q x

High card value 9.

The complete bidding would now be:

Bidder	Responder
1 ♠	2 ◇
3 ◇ [1]	3 ♡ [2]
3 N T [3]	5 ◇ [4]
6 ◇ [5]	Pass

[1] The correct bid.

[2] A Slam Invitation. Responder's hand is equivalent to a fine original bid.

[3] Playing safe. Responder's three-heart bid might not have been a Slam Invitation, but merely a desire to reach three notrump.

[4] A second Slam Try. Four diamonds would not have been passed.

[5] Accepts the Invitation. Does not show the club control, as he is not interested in seven.

Type 5.

♠ x x x　　♡ x x　　♢ A Q x x　　♣ A K x x

High card value 9.

This is the type of hand which accounts for many hard-luck stories. Should the Responder immediately bid two notrump, his partner, holding the King and a small heart, is likely to bid game in notrump, whereupon a heart lead might quickly defeat the contract. However, should Responder bid two diamonds and the Original Bidder then bid two notrump, a three-notrump contract would be safe, since a heart lead would be up to declarer's King of hearts. Incidentally, should partner's rebid over two diamonds be two spades, we would bid four spades.

In all the preceding examples, Responder has held a good hand, and we wish to emphasize that the response of two of a lower ranking suit is a constructive, not a weakness, bid. The only exception occurs when Responder is weak in high cards, but has substantial playing strength in his suit. For example, your partner opens with one spade. You hold

♠ x　　♡ x x x　　♢ K J 10 9 x x　　♣ x x x

High card value 2½.

You do not fancy the idea of playing one spade, and respond with two diamonds. If the Bidder rebids to two spades, you must pass and let him take his medicine. If he bids two hearts, you have improved matters and you also pass. If he bids two notrump, you bid three diamonds—a definite Sign-off.

CHAPTER XXXII

The Four Aces Jump Two-Over-One

IN OTHER Bridge systems the Jump response of two in a higher ranking suit is used to show a pretty fair hand with which the Responder thinks he can probably make game. This response not only crowds the bidding, but is totally unnecessary. In addition to this, it robs the player of the very useful specialized Two-Over-One bid which we have invented and adopted as an integral part of our system.

The response of two in a higher ranking suit is seldom used, but the few hands which do warrant its use are of great importance. It is used for one purpose by a player who has passed, and for another purpose by a player who has not passed.

BY A PLAYER WHO HAS PASSED

When made by a player who has passed, it conveys the message: "Partner, if you have a bid, even though it may be shaded, we must continue to game."

Consider the following hand:

♠ K Q J 10 x   ♡ K x x x   ◇ Q J x   ♣ x

High card value 7.

This is a borderline hand which we do not bid originally, as we fear a misfit, should partner hold a club hand. Accord-

251

ingly, if partner opens with a club following our pass, we bid one spade, still worrying about the misfit. However, if partner opens with a diamond or a heart, we have no such fears, and by means of a bid of two spades convey the message: "Partner, even though you have shaded your Opening bid requirements, nevertheless, I am forcing you to continue the bidding to game."

♠ K J x x x x   ♡ A x x x x   ◇ x   ♣ x

High card value 5½.

We pass this hand originally and partner opens with one heart. We now bid two spades, as we are certain of a splendid fit. If he opens with one diamond or one club, we bid only one spade.

Some players may feel that if they pass a doubtful bid originally, they should automatically make a Two-Over-One response. This is decidedly not the case, and even though we pass such a hand as

♠ A K x x   ♡ A x x   ◇ J x x   ♣ J x x

High card value 9.

we bid only one spade over partner's Third- or Fourth-Hand Opening in another suit.

BY A PLAYER WHO HAS NOT PASSED

When made by a player who has not passed, it conveys a different message: "Partner, my hand is so strong, that if you have opened a psychic, bid two notrump, whereupon we will continue to game. If you have a bid, even a minimum, you must take some other action. We will continue either to a Small or a Grand Slam."

The following hands illustrate this bid:

Bidder	Responder
♠ x x	♠ A K Q J x x
♡ x x x	♡ A x
◇ x x	◇ x
♣ J x x x x	♣ A x x x

The bidding:

Bidder	Responder
1 ♣ [1]	2 ♠ [2]
2 N T [3]	4 ♠ [4]

[1] All original psychics should show length in the suit bid.
[2] Certain of game, even though the Opening bid is a psychic.
[3] Showing the Opening bid was a psychic.
[4] Contracting for game.

Bidder	Responder
♠ x	♠ A K Q J x x
♡ x x x	♡ A x
◇ A K x x	◇ x
♣ K Q J x x	♣ A x x x

The bidding:

Bidder	Responder
1 ♣ [1]	2 ♠
3 ♣ [2]	3 ♠ [3]
3 N T [4]	4 ♣ [5]
4 ◇ [6]	7 ♣ [7]

[1] A proper Opening one-club.

[2] Shows the original bid was not a psychic, and at the same time indicates a five-card club suit.

[3] Taking things easy.

[4] Showing that the original bid was minimum. Responder cannot pass, since the two-spade bid is forcing to a Slam.

[5] Showing club support.

[6] A control-showing bid. Once Responder raises clubs, Bidder's hand is improved.

[7] There is no need for any further exchange of information.

Bidder	Responder
♠ x	♠ A K Q J x
♡ x x x	♡ A K Q J x
◇ A K x x	◇ x
♣ K Q J x x	♣ x x

The bidding:

Bidder	Responder
1 ♣	2 ♠
3 ♣	3 ♡ [1]
3 N T [2]	4 ♡ [3]
5 ♡ [4]	6 ♡ [5]

[1] Showing his second suit.

[2] No real support for either of Responder's suits.

[3] Rebidding his hearts. The Bidder cannot pass.

[4] A proper Raise.

[5] Responder does not bid seven, since Bidder's minimum bidding has clearly shown that he does not hold both the minor-suit Aces.

Bidder	Responder
♠ A x x	♠ x
♡ A x x	♡ K Q J 10 x x
◊ x x x	◊ A K x
♣ A J x x	♣ K Q x

The bidding:

Bidder	Responder
1 ♣	2 ♡
3 N T [1]	4 ♡ [2]
4 ♠ [3]	5 ◊ [4]
6 ♡ [5]	7 ♡ [6]

[1] Merely indicates a balanced original bid. Remember, a two-notrump bid would show a psychic.

[2] Rebidding his suit.

[3] A control-showing bid.

[4] Another control-showing bid.

[5] Up to this point Bidder has merely shown a minimum hand. His three Aces must be of tremendous value, and hence he now suggests a Grand Slam.

[6] Responder has now located the Ace of hearts.

CHAPTER XXXIII

The Three-Card Minor-Suit Bid

UNDER the Four Aces System, the three-card minor-suit bid is our general utility man. It is neither used nor intended as a psychic, and is employed only with a hand which is a compulsory bid (high card value 9½ or more). It is used when we have no biddable suit.

The following hands will illustrate its use:

♠ A x x   ♡ J x x x   ◇ A x x   ♣ A x x

High card value 9½.

Just too strong to pass—bid one club. With this hand, rebids should be made in minimums and only in response to Forcing or near-Forcing bids. The reader should bear in mind that if partner immediately raises his club suit to two, he has no right to bid again, nor should he fear to play that contract. If the initial response is one heart, raise to two; if one diamond or one spade, bid one notrump.

With slightly stronger hands, such as

♠ Q x x x   ♡ A Q x   ◇ K x x   ♣ A Q x

High card value 11.

where we are just too weak for an Opening one-notrump, we may rebid more strongly in a manner commensurate

256

with our additional strength. Now, if partner responds with two clubs, we bid two notrump as an invitation to game; while if he responds with a heart, diamond or spade, we give him a single Raise in his suit, hoping that he will find a second bid. If his response is one notrump, we pass.

The final class of hands which we open with a three-card minor are those which are too strong for one no-trump and not strong enough for two notrump, such as

♠ A K x   ♡ Q x x x   ♢ A 10 x   ♣ A K x

High card value 14 with 7 honors.

which we open with one club. Now, whatever response partner makes, we shall take appropriate strong action, intending to reach game and in many instances to invite or even bid a Slam.

CHAPTER XXXIV

Psychic Bids

IN THIS chapter we enter the field of deceptive bidding. There is no necessity for a player to make use of such bids, but should he desire to employ them occasionally—either defensively, in an effort to embarrass the opponents and to prevent them from reaching the proper final contract, or offensively, in an effort to convey a confused picture of his hand and mislead the defense—it is essential that there be method in his madness. Just as he employs a complete and recognized portfolio of normal bidding, his psychics should be catalogued, so that the misinformation conveyed by them will not act as a boomerang to his own side.

The reckless psychic in a Bridge game is likely to prove a Frankenstein monster and turn against its maker. There are, however, a few psychics which serve to add zest to the game, to keep all the players alert, and which, if intelligently used, involve very little risk. In their use, as in the employment of all other advanced bids, great care must be taken. Just as there are certain players with whom you should overbid and others with whom you should underbid, so there are certain players with whom you should *never bid a psychic.* Such players are those who never recognize one or those who always suspect one.

The first defensive psychic to consider is the one made

as an Opening bid. Such a bid, of course, should never be
made in fourth position, while the best position to venture
one is third hand. The risks you take with an Opening
third-hand psychic are (1) that fourth hand, instead of
disclosing his strength, will pass and that your partner
with a fair hand will respond to your psychic, whereupon
you will be doubled and severely penalized, and (2) that
partner will not realize that you have bid a psychic and
will double the opponents' declaration, whereupon they
may redouble and score a great many more points than if
the bidding had been normal.

In most cases it is not difficult to recognize when your
partner has bid a psychic. For instance, you deal and pass,
holding

♠ A x x   ♡ K x x   ◊ A x x   ♣ x x x x

High card value 8.

Your partner, in third position, bids a diamond, fourth
hand doubles, and you redouble to show you have passed
a strong hand. Second hand now bids one spade, your partner passes, fourth hand bids three spades, you pass, second
hand bids four spades which is passed around to you. At
this point, unless both opponents are insane, it should be
obvious that your partner's bid was a psychic. Therefore,
if you should now elect to double, you may attach no blame
to your partner because the opponents' display of great
strength has clearly shown the character of his Opening
bid.

Another situation, however, is more serious. Suppose
you are third hand holding

♠ x x x   ♡ x x x   ◊ x x x   ♣ x x x x

and bid one club. Fourth hand passes. Your partner, the

dealer, with a maximum original pass (a high card value of 8½ or 9), now bids two notrump, second hand passes, you pass, and fourth hand doubles for business. The trap is sprung, and there is no escape from the tremendous penalty of a set of five or six tricks. But, of course, you have "saved" a game!

Let us consider an even sadder case. You are third hand and hold

♠ x   ♡ J x x x   ◇ x x x x   ♣ x x x x

You fear that the opponents can score a game and probably a Slam. You feel that your only chance to defend successfully is to confuse them as much as possible. With that in mind, you open the bidding with one spade. Fourth hand doubles, your partner holds

♠ Q x x x x   ♡ Q x   ◇ A x x x   ♣ x x

and jumps to three spades, the proper bid over the adverse double. The opponents double, and you can do nothing but squirm and suffer a penalty of at least six tricks.

These two hands are given as horrible examples. The psychic bid, in the first illustration, is not only very dangerous, but is quite pointless because it is extremely unlikely that it will deceive the opponents, while in the second example, the psychic is almost suicidal.

In our opinion, an Opening psychic bid in third position should be, in all cases, of a somewhat constructive nature and should give partner some definite information as to the distribution of the bidding hand. An unjustifiable risk is taken if made in a suit of less than four cards.

In discussing this subject the feature of vulnerability has not been mentioned because the only rule for vulnerable defensive psychics is—DON'T BID THEM.

The following are examples of perfectly proper Opening third-hand psychics:

♠ x   ♡ x x x   ◇ x x x   ♣ K x x x x x

High card value 2.

Bid one club. This bid is not likely to lead to any serious trouble and will occasionally, scare an opponent away from game or Slam.

♠ Q x x x x   ♡ Q x x x x   ◇ x x   ♣ x

High card value 2.

Bid one spade. This bid also may keep your opponents from a game bid and at the same time involves slight risk of severe loss.

Digressing from the subject of third-hand psychics, let us consider the following hand:

♠ A J x x x   ♡ K x   ◇ x x x   ♣ x x

Obviously this hand is suitable for a third-hand semi-psychic, or lead-directing bid. Many players occasionally bid such hands in first or second position. We strongly disapprove of this practice. If you open the bidding with such a hand in first or second position, your future course of action becomes confused and uncertain. If your partner makes a Forcing response, you would fear that he might undertake an unmakable Slam if you rebid, while if you should pass, you might miss a game. Furthermore, if the bidding becomes competitive, your partner may double the opponents at a contract they can easily make. In return for this you have gained the doubtful advantage of having made the first bid. We cannot warn too strongly against *first- and second-hand semi-psychics.*

For a first-hand psychic your hand should be so bad that you can afford to pass partner's response. For instance, having dealt and holding

♠ x x   ♡ x x   ◊ x x   ♣ J x x x x x

you might bid one club on the theory that since two opponents and but one partner are to be heard from, the chances are greater that the adversaries may bid and make a game or Slam than that your partner holds enough strength to defeat either contract. In such case the psychic is likely to deter a Slam bid and may even prevent a game bid. However, with such a hand in second position it is advisable to pass, due to the fact that as one opponent has previously passed, there is an even chance that your partner holds the best hand. Therefore, follow this rigid rule —NEVER BID A SECOND-HAND PSYCHIC.

Let us now discuss the Defensive Psychic Overcall. Consider the following hand:

♠ x x   ♡ x x   ◊ x   ♣ K Q J x x x x

High card value 3½.

Dealer opens the bidding with a spade, heart or diamond at our right. With this hand many writers recommend a Bluff One Notrump or a Bluff Double. We believe such a bid is pointless. Against good players it will prove to be ineffective, while poor players may reach the wrong contract without interference on your part. Under Overcalls we have discussed the Jump Overcall which is similar to a Pre-emptive bid. The advocates of the Bluff Notrump or Bluff Double maintain that if your bluff is doubled your club suit offers a safe retreat, and that if your escape bid of two clubs is doubled you are delighted that a small penalty has been exchanged for an adverse game. But suppose you do bid a Bluff Notrump and after being doubled by the next player that you run to two clubs, the only thing you will have accomplished is the exposure of your weakness, which will encourage your opponents confidently to continue the contracting until a game or Slam bid is reached. Suppose your Bluff Notrump is doubled and you then make a four-club Pre-emptive bid. Your Psychic is now completely exposed and at the same time you have given the player sitting over you the opportunity to double your notrump, thereby showing his partner that he has a good hand. How different if your first bid is four clubs! You will then have shut out the opportunity for the preliminary exchange of information between your opponents and if they risk an overcall it is not unlikely that they will fail to reach the proper final contract. For these reasons with a weak freakish hand, we advise against the use of a Psychic and strongly recommend the immediate Pre-emptive Jump Overcall.

One of the best opportunities for a Defensive Psychic occurs when you fear that the opponents may bid and make a Slam. In this situation the bid will at times prevent a Slam bid which otherwise would be reached. The fake lead-directing bid is perhaps the most valuable Psychic of this sort.

To illustrate—you are Fourth Hand. Dealer bids one spade. Second Hand bids two hearts and Third Hand three hearts—a positive cue bid inviting a Slam. You hold

♠ x x   ♡ A x x x x x   ◇ x x   ♣ x x x

High card value 3.

With this hand you are certain that the opponents can

make a Slam. You therefore bid four diamonds over the three hearts. If the original bidder has a good diamond suit in addition to his good spade suit, he will double the four diamonds for business. The next two players pass. You run to four hearts. It is now probable that the original bidder will reason as follows: "Why did Fourth Hand bid four diamonds? In all likelihood to tell his partner that he can safely lead a diamond against a Slam contract because he can ruff. This seems very likely because I have so many diamonds. Therefore, I should not contract for a Slam."

The following hand was played by Mr. Harold S. Vanderbilt, sitting North:

♠ Q J ♡ x ◇ A K Q J 10 9 8 7 6 ♣ x

High card value 8.

East and West were vulnerable. North and South were not. East dealt and bid one spade, to which West replied by bidding three spades. North passed, knowing that he would have another chance to bid. East now bid four clubs, inviting a Slam, to which West responded with four diamonds. At this point, Mr. Vanderbilt realized that as his Queen-Jack would drop, the opponents could probably make a Grand Slam in spades, and being certain that they could make a Small Slam, he wished to play the hand defensively at seven diamonds, at which contract his loss would be limited to 550 points. Therefore, he bid five clubs, which was promptly doubled by East. South and West passed. North bid five diamonds. East passed. West bid five hearts. North passed. East bid six spades. West passed. North now bid seven diamonds and East doubled, feeling certain that North's club bid had shown a void suit and indicated the lead which would defeat seven spades. The other three hands were:

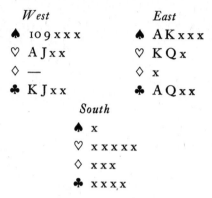

As Dummy was able to ruff one of his two spades, he went down only three tricks for a net loss of 350 points, whereas East and West had a laydown for a vulnerable Grand Slam.

A frequent type of valuable Defensive Psychic may be employed in the following situation: You are Fourth Hand and the bidding has been: one club, one heart, one spade. You hold

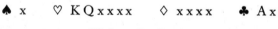

High card value 6.

You foresee that the opponents will probably play the hand at spades and that you will have the lead. You are prepared to defend as high as five hearts and would venture six, were it not for the fact that you will very likely be able to defeat five spades, particularly if you can lead the opponents to mark you with whatever high diamonds they lack. Accordingly, rather than raise your partner's heart suit you bid two diamonds. If partner raises, you

can always go back to hearts. Having pushed the opponents to five spades, you lead the King of hearts. If
they have to take a diamond finesse it is almost certain
that it will be taken the wrong way, thereby giving you the
trick necessary to defeat the contract. Furthermore, such
bids frequently cause the opponents optimistically to contract for a Slam. Suppose the original bidder is void in
hearts, has the Ace-Queen of diamonds, good support in
his partner's spade suit and the King-Queen-Jack of clubs.
He will probably count no diamond losers, and so bid six
spades, which contract will be defeated if your partner
holds the King of diamonds.

DEFENSIVE PSYCHICS WHEN YOUR PARTNER HAS OPENED THE BIDDING

Such bids, in general, are not advisable because in most
instances your partner's Opening bid indicates sufficient
strength to prevent the opponents making a game or Slam
contract. However, there is one situation when such a
psychic may prove to be profitable: namely, when your
partner opens the bidding and second hand, either by a
double or a bid in your partner's suit, shows a very strong
hand and your holding is so weak that you feel certain
that the opponents, if unmolested, will bid and make a
game. In this situation, you may even go so far as to bid
the short suit in which you think the opponents are most
likely to score game, since your partner should know that
if you have a good hand you would redouble rather than
bid. In this instance, we do not approve of a bluff or
psychic redouble because such a bid leaves the contracting
at a low level which will permit the opponents advan-
tageously to exchange whatever information they desire.
The following hand was bid by Mr. Waldemar von Zedt-

witz and Mr. Edward Hymes, Jr., and illustrates the use
of this short-suit bid:

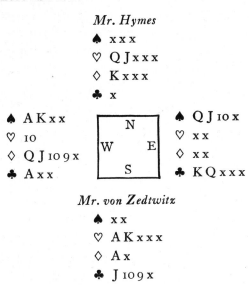

Mr. Hymes

♠ x x x
♡ Q J x x x
◊ K x x x
♣ x

♠ A K x x
♡ 10
◊ Q J 10 9 x
♣ A x x

♠ Q J 10 x
♡ x x
◊ x x
♣ K Q x x x

Mr. von Zedtwitz

♠ x x
♡ A K x x x
◊ A x
♣ J 10 9 x

Mr. von Zedtwitz, South, dealt and bid one heart which
West promptly doubled, whereupon Mr. Hymes, rather
than raise hearts immediately, bid one spade. East probably should have doubled for business but instead bid two
clubs. Mr. von Zedtwitz passed and West bid two diamonds. Mr. Hymes, still afraid that his opponents would
discover their fit in spades, now repeated his psychic by
bidding two spades, East passed. Of course, at this point
an alert player could have exposed the psychic by doubling,
but by this time East was distrustful of his partner's
original Double. Mr. von Zedtwitz passed, and West now
bid three clubs. Mr. Hymes showed heart support by
bidding three hearts, East bid four clubs, South four
hearts, West five clubs, North and East passed, South

doubled and all passed. The contract was defeated two tricks.

This hand was played in a team-of-four match, and at the other table Mr. Louis H. Watson and Mr. A. Mitchell Barnes, sitting East and West, bid and made four spades with the same hands that the opponents played at five clubs.

ATTACKING PSYCHICS

Attacking Psychics are generally bid for the purpose of misleading the opponents in their defense of the hand. An elementary Attacking Psychic is the following:

♠ A x x x x   ♡ A K J x x   ◇ —   ♣ A x x

High card value 11½.

As dealer, we bid one spade and partner responds with two spades. While this hand will almost certainly produce a Small Slam in spades we are anxious to eliminate a dangerous feature—a club lead. In the event that partner holds a hand such as the following:

♠ K x x x   ♡ Q x   ◇ K x x   ♣ x x x x

High card value 5.

a club lead will almost certainly defeat our contract, in the event that spades do not break. Accordingly, before bidding six spades we make a lead-misdirecting bid of three clubs. The three-club bid is a Temporary Force. Having made the club bid, our next bid of course would be six spades.

The more common lead-misdirecting bids occur when you are preparing for notrump. Suppose partner has bid one spade, and you hold

♠ Q x   ♡ K J x x   ◇ A Q x x   ♣ x x x

High card value 7½.

You decide that you should play the hand at game and preferably in notrump. In the event you are declarer, you probably will make three notrump, provided the opponents do not know of your weakness in clubs. Accordingly, instead of making a normal bid of two diamonds, you bid two clubs. If partner bids two spades you bid two notrump, and if he bids three notrump it will then be unlikely that the damaging club lead will be the opening. Of course if such lead-misdirecting bids are frequently made, your opponents will not be fooled and will outguess you by opening the suit that you have bid. Should this happen, the answer is to become honest and bid the suit you want led. We know one of the keenest Bridge psychologists who frequently played with and against a certain player, also a psychologist but not a keen one. He kept a record of his attempts to cause that player to make the desired lead. In 20 instances he found that he had succeeded 18 times. Of course, opportunities for making such bids occur rarely. It required several months of play to provide the 20 cases.

In making such bids, you should exercise great caution. For instance, suppose you hold

♠ x   ♡ A x   ◇ K x x   ♣ A K Q x x x x

High card value 11.

You say to yourself: "Ah, I can make three notrump if I can prevent a spade lead," and with that in mind you bid one spade. Your partner now bids three spades. You bid three notrump. Partner bids four spades. You bid five clubs. Your partner bids six spades, which is doubled and the severe penalty you suffer is aggravated by the realization that you could easily have made three notrump. Therefore, as the first rule for such bids we recommend: Do not bid them in a major suit. If you bid them in a minor and get into difficulty, you can always go back to your own or your partner's higher ranking suit at the same level. Secondly, make them only when you have a safety factor. For instance, reverting to a previous example:

♠ A x x x x   ♡ A K J x x   ◇ —   ♣ A x x

High card value 11½.

You bid one spade. Partner bids two spades. You bid three clubs. Even though partner now carries you to seven clubs, you can return to spades and should have a very good play for seven.

SUMMARY

Psychics, like all other bids, should be part of a complete and coherent system or method. To that end we recommend the following simple rules:

(1) Do not open with a defensive psychic in second position.

(2) Opening defensive psychics should never be made in a suit of less than four cards.

(3) Do not open with semi-psychics, or lead-directing bids, in first or second position.

(4) Do not use a Bluff Notrump or Bluff Double over an Opening bid when you can properly make an immediate Defensive Jump Overcall. If an opponent opens the bidding, there is little to be gained and much to be lost by bidding a Bluff Notrump or by doubling, since such tactics, while occasionally successful, will cause your partner to disbelieve you when you really have a good hand. Further-

more, a psychic double or Bluff notrump still permits the opponents to exchange information at a low level. We believe that the most satisfactory defense with a weak hand and a long suit is immediately to pre-empt with as high a bid in the long suit as you dare make; the alternative is to pass and take your medicine.

(5) In competitive bidding, situations frequently arise in which psychic bids may be made in an effort to obtain the contract at a lower level than would otherwise be the case. When such bids are made, you should have strength in your partner's suit and the suit bid psychicly should be lower in rank than that suit, since otherwise he might continue to bid your psychic suit and not realize the situation in time to escape disaster.

(6) Attacking psychics are made in an effort to confuse the defense. They are most frequently employed when you wish to play the hand at three notrump and are used, thus: over partner's Opening suit bid, respond with a lower-valued suit, preferably a minor in which you are rather weak, on the theory that it may prevent a damaging lead. A similar bid may be made when on the way to a Slam, but in both instances care should be taken that the psychic suit is lower in rank than the one at which you may safely play the hand; otherwise your partner, not realizing that your bid was a psychic, might carry the bidding too high.

(7) A final word of advice in the use of psychics: Do not use them too frequently, as they will lose their effectiveness and cause your partners to mistrust all your bids. Against players who bid them habitually the best defense is not to parry in kind, but to adhere to normal sound bidding.

CHAPTER XXXV

The Psychology of Bridge

A GALLERY OF BRIDGE PLAYERS

THE psychology of Bridge involves a study of players, rather than hands, and just as hands may be classified, players, too, fall naturally into categories.

With this in mind we present a typical gallery of Bridge players, classified according to their distinguishing faults, virtues or idiosyncrasies. When we come to the chapter on Partnership we shall refer to this gallery, in order to show how the winning player modifies his game with various partners:

THE BURDEN BEARER

The Burden Bearer in most cases is a good player who bids on the psychological principle that it is advisable to take the strain of difficult decisions from his partner's shoulders whenever possible. For instance, his partner raises his one-spade bid to two, and although his hand properly calls for a rebid to three spades, he will jump to four on the theory that should he bid three, it would leave a difficult and almost unnecessary decision to his partner.

So long as the Burden Bearer confines himself to making things easy for his partner, he will be a winning player, but unless he is careful, he is likely to acquire the deadly *nursing* habit, and become a Nursemaid.

THE NURSEMAID

This player is always in deathly fear that his partner either will or has made a mistake, and, accordingly, acts to anticipate or counteract it.

Practically all the players whose portraits hang in this gallery suffer in some form from this habit.

THE NOTRUMPIST

The notrumpist believes that nearly all game hands should be played at three notrump, and furthermore, that he has been divinely appointed to play them. At the first opportunity he bids some number of notrump, and irrespective of how often his partner takes him out, he is almost certain to go back to his favorite declaration.

There are two types of notrumpists, but both are undesirable partners.

The first type, while bullish about his own notrumps, is terribly bearish about his partner's, and, accordingly, if his partner bids notrump, he will take him out in all sorts of ridiculous ways in order to find a better spot.

The second type is almost as enthusiastic about his partner's notrump contracts as his own, and while naturally he is a little disappointed at not being able to play the notrump himself, still he will raise to the limit rather than make a proper Takeout.

The notrumpist is arbitrarily an overbidder and so may obtain good results with a cautious underbidding partner, but he is bound to get into serious difficulties when playing with one of his own ilk.

THE TRAPPER

This player bids in such a manner as to trap his partner. In the early stages of the bidding he is inclined to underbid his hand; eventually, his partner makes what should be the final bid for the partnership, but the trapper now revalues his hand, decides that he has underbid, and makes one more bid, which is the trap.

The following are examples of Trap bids:

Partner	Trapper
1 ♠	3 ♠ [1]
4 ♠ [2]	5 ♠ [3]

[1] This bid, of course, is forcing to game, but suggests Slam possibilities only if partner invites it.

[2] Partner quite properly expects that this will close the bidding.

[3] The trapper now shows excess values by this bad bid. *Comment:* He could have conveyed this same picture of strength without getting beyond game, by giving a Slam Invitational Game Force on his first bid.

Partner	Trapper
Pass	2 N T [1]
3 N T [2]	4 N T [3]

[1] Inviting partner to bid three notrump with as much as a Queen and Jack.

[2] Expecting this to be the final bid.

[3] Inexcusable.
Comment: The trapper undoubtedly should have bid three notrump in the first place.

Partner	*Trapper*
1 ♡	4 ♡ [1]
6 ♡ [2]	7 ♡ [3]

[1] A game bid showing strong distributional and moderate high card support for the opening one-heart bid.

[2] Clearly willing to play six but not expecting seven.

[3] Inexcusable—the usual apology for this trap is: "Partner, if you had bid only five hearts, I would have bid six."

The Trapper fails to realize that while five always invites six, six, in this instance, definitely does not invite seven.

The following bids, while apparently similar, are not traps and are perfectly proper:

Bidder	*Responder*
1 ♠	2 ♡ [1]
4 ♡ [2]	5 ♡ [3]

[1] An Exploratory bid which is forcing for one round.

[2] A very strong rebid, clearly suggesting Slam possibilities.

[3] Since the two-heart bid has been Exploratory and not limiting, the five-heart bid may now properly suggest a Slam.

Bidder	*Responder*
2 N T	6 N T
7 N T [1]	

[1] Perfectly justifiable, since, in this instance, the six-no-trump bid definitely invited seven.

The final test as to whether a bid is a trap is the answer to the question, "Does my partner expect his bid to be passed?" In the event that he does expect you to pass, and you make a further bid, you have definitely trapped him.

THE MICROMETER

This player believes in mathematical exactitude and precision in bidding. He derives no glow of satisfaction in bidding and making a doubtful game, since he feels that, to be precise, he should have stopped one trick lower. On the other hand, successful fulfillment of a three-spade contract is enormously gratifying to him.

Furthermore, this player believes in a complete exchange of information, and even though he and his partner have found a fit in a major suit, he will continue to show other suits so as to be sure that the opponents will know the best defense.

THE DOUBLER

The Doubler does more to upset his partner's equilibrium than almost any other player.

In the first place, when the opponents bid a game or a Slam, the Doubler is inclined to take action whenever he thinks that a trick in his partner's hand will defeat the adverse contract. For instance, the Doubler with an Ace, will double a six-bid, expecting that his partner can take another trick, or will double a four-bid with two Aces and a King, expecting that his three high cards will all take tricks and that his partner will surely be able to win another one.

These instances are bad enough, since the opponents may redouble and make their contract with an overtrick, but when his unfortunate partner happens to put in a sound but highly distributional overcall, then woe betide him, because the Doubler will expect him to take two or three defensive tricks against the opponents' contract. Here the scores for redoubled overtricks mount to staggering figures. Of course, the unfortunate partner with a hopeless hand for defensive purposes might take out the Double, but if he did so he would probably find that the Doubler really had the opponents set for once in his miserable life.

In competitive bidding, the Doubler is even more dangerous to his partner because his theory is to bid as much as he can and then double to make his partner stop. As a result, when he can make game himself he doubles the opponents for a one-trick set, or when his partner could defend at small cost he doubles the opponents' successful contract.

Of course, when we cite the faults of the Doubler we do not mean to imply that one should never double, but merely that in doubling you should have a more important objective than a mere one-trick set.

THE GALLANT DEFENDER

The Gallant Defender labors under the delusion that he has been predestined to save all games. Whenever he has an opportunity to save game, he rushes into the breach ignoring the possibility that he might incur a tremendous penalty or that the opponents might not make their contract. Of course, he does have his moment of grandeur when by some miracle his bid is not set and he makes a game that no one else would think of bidding.

THE GENERALISSIMO

The Generalissimo goes one step further than the

Nursemaid. He makes decisions on the theory that he is above all rules of the game, and that what he does must be right.

On this hand the Generalissimo will pass his partner's opening one-spade bid, holding

♠ K x x x   ♡ K x x x   ◊ x x   ♣ Q x x

because he has decided arbitrarily that there is no game in the hand, and therefore that there is no point in getting beyond one spade. However, with a slightly better hand which includes the club King instead of the Queen he is very likely to bid three spades, following his optimistic decision that there is game in the hand.

His Slam bidding is even more erratic because he is inclined arbitrarily to mark desired cards in his partner's hand whenever he feels like it.

THE LEAPER

The Leaper is similar to the Generalissimo in that his erratic bidding is based entirely on his arbitrary decision as to what the final contract should be. However, whereas the Generalissimo, on some hands, is very likely to give his partner considerable information by means of scientific developing bids, the Leaper does not do so, because his bidding is characterized by a series of wild leaps and jumps.

While this bounding style interferes but slightly with successful game bidding, it is completely hopeless for Slam purposes.

THE MAGICIAN

The Magician believes that he can cause tricks to materialize out of thin air, just as a conjuror takes rabbits from a high hat. Whenever he expects to be the declarer he is prepared to and does overbid from one to three tricks.

The Magician is usually a pretty good card player but unfortunately nullifies his own natural advantage, due to the fact that he utilizes his skill to hold the set to one instead of three at impossible contracts.

THE RABBIT OR PASSER

The Rabbit is deathly afraid of being set. As a result, he is continually stopping at such contracts as two notrump, three spades, or four clubs, and while he occasionally obtains good results, he is a sure loser in the long run.

THE PSYCHER

This player feels that he must outwit his opponents on every hand. His psychics are bid so frequently that they scarcely embarrass the opponents at all.

As he continually bids them with most unsuitable hands, his unfortunate partner is always in the dark and can never satisfactorily approach a final contract when the psycher really has a good hand.

THE MULE

A Mule cannot understand a denial, and irrespective of how often you show him an unwillingness to play his denomination he will always return to it like a moth to the flame, and, in addition, will never allow his partner to sign-off.

Suppose the Mule holds

♠ AQ7432   ♡ x   ◇ Kxx   ♣ Axx

and makes a sound Opening one-spade bid. When his partner bids two hearts, he makes the proper bid of two spades, but now pity the unfortunate partner with a void of spades and seven or eight hearts who persists in the error of his ways and bids three hearts. Although a normal player would recognize the misfit and pass immediately, the Mule sees only his own hand and bids either three spades or three notrump. Whichever his choice, if partner now bids four hearts, the Mule will still go back to spades.

With this particular hand, the Mule's rebidding would be based primarily on optimism about his own spade suit combined with pessimism about his partner's hearts.

In other instances, it might be caused by annoyance at his partner's seemingly obstinate refusal to permit him to play the hand. For instance, the Mule holds

$$\spadesuit \text{ A 10 x} \qquad \heartsuit \text{ A x} \qquad \diamondsuit \text{ A J x x} \qquad \clubsuit \text{ A x x x}$$

and makes a sound opening one-notrump bid. Partner responds with two hearts, and the Mule bids two notrump. Partner now signs off with three hearts, and the undaunted Mule bids three notrump, reasoning, as a mule would, that if partner has six hearts to the King-Queen-Jack, game of course will be a laydown. Unfortunately, partner, who sees his own hand, cannot find the King and is forced to bid four hearts. The Mule is now really annoyed, and without realizing that the four-heart bid indicates that notrump is an impossible contract, obstinately bids four notrump.

It is an interesting feature of Bridge psychology that whenever a player possesses idiosyncrasies, he is inclined, without realizing it, to mark his partner with the same faults. This is particularly true of the Mule and most of his obstinate rebidding is based on the assumption that his partner's rebids are equally stubborn.

THE SLAMO-MANIAC

This player believes that Slams grow on bushes, waiting to be picked by the player who bids them, and he is likely to grab at one on the slightest provocation only to find that he has a handful of thorns.

The occasional fulfillment of such a contract due to poor defense more than compensates him for the loss of ten games.

THE STEADY FREE BIDDER

This player does not believe in passing, and is inclined to open such hands as

♠ xxx   ♡ A K xx   ◇ Kxx   ♣ xxx

or

♠ xx   ♡ A J xxxx   ◇ Kxx   ♣ xx

with one heart on the theory that if partner has a weak hand he has shown him the right lead, and also has intimidated the opponents. Of course, if partner has a good hand the Steady Free Bidder has completely fixed himself for all subsequent bidding.

While his Opening bids are bad, his overcalls are even worse. The possibility that the opponents will get too high if he keeps still never occurs to him, and holding two Aces and a King, he will always double or overcall. Such bids not only do him no good, but frequently cost him tremendous penalties.

THE RESCUER

The Rescuer usually is a Steady Free Bidder himself and since he is inclined to make overcalls on high cards, regardless of playing strength, he automatically believes the same of his partner.

He is an optimist about his own hand and always expects his partner to fit any suit he may hold.

If his partner is doubled, the Rescuer automatically assumes the worst. Three small cards of his partner's suit mean nothing to him. For instance, suppose he is Junior and holds:

♠ x x   ♡ x x x   ◇ x x x   ♣ A K Q x x

The bidding proceeds: One spade by Bidder, two diamonds by Senior, his partner, and double by Responder. At this point, the Rescuer bids three clubs. He does not realize that his high cards in clubs will take tricks at diamonds. He does not realize that his three small diamonds clearly indicate that the player to his left will have either a singleton or a void. He does not realize that three clubs is one trick higher than two diamonds. The only thing that goes through his mind is that his partner has been doubled and he must save him.

THE HOG

The hog wants to play every hand. If his partner bids notrump, the hog takes out in a suit; if his partner bids a suit; the hog goes to notrump.

CHAPTER XXXVI

Partnership

SUCCESSFUL bidding depends to a great extent upon partnership confidence and co-operation. Even when this is present, perfect results will not always be attained, and the occasional bad results will be attributable to faulty or unfortunate bidding by one or both partners.

Winning players use their bad results to improve their own game. Each partner tries to determine how he, himself, might have prevented the catastrophe. As an example, in the finals of an important tournament, two players, having a very fine partnership, held the following hands:

North (Dealer)	South
♠ K Q 9 2	♠ A 7 6
♡ A K J 5	♡ 8 7 4 2
◇ Q 10	◇ K J 6 3 2
♣ Q J 6	♣ 5

The bidding was:

North	East	South	West
1 ♠	Pass	2 ♠	Pass
Pass	Pass		

While only three spades could be made, it was obvious that four hearts could not have been beaten.

A casual observer might have thought that neither had noticed this fact. Rather than upset their partnership by any immediate discussion, they decided to ignore it temporarily. (Any argument between partners is certain to have a bad effect on their bidding and play of the next few hands.) As soon as the session of play was concluded, there was an immediate conference on the hand.

Unlike the common instances where a player sees only his partner's faults, each was insistent upon blaming himself. South apologized for not having bid two diamonds, saying, that he realized his hand warranted that bid, but had arbitrarily become pessimistic and hence merely bid two spades. Had South bid two diamonds, the bidding, of course, would have proceeded, two hearts by North, three hearts by South, and four hearts by North.

North, on the other hand, blamed himself, stating that he had refused to make a second bid after the two-spade response because he also had become pessimistic. North's opinion was that he should have bid two notrump over the two-spade response, whereupon South would have bid three diamonds, North three hearts, and South four hearts. In other words, each player realized that he could have prevented the final error, and determined to avoid a repetition of his mistake.

Unfortunately, this attitude is taken by very few players. Usually, the discussion occurs immediately after the error. Each player is so intent upon pointing out his partner's stupidity that he is unable to see his own mistake and repeats it on the next occasion.

Our advice to any student of the game who wishes to become a better player is: Cheerfully accept the blame for any error your partner may accuse you of, with a mental reservation to study the hand at your leisure. Study the hand in the following manner:

First, determine whether you could have prevented the catastrophe. If this is the case, resolve to avoid a repetition of the error. However, if after complete analysis, you decide that you are not at fault, then discuss the matter with your partner. A good line of approach is: "Jim, remember that hand we had last night where we reached the wrong contract? I was somewhat to blame, but at the same time I think you made it pretty difficult for me—let me show you the hand."

Hours after the incident, almost anyone will listen and be inclined to recognize and admit his own error. Discussions of this type are essential to the formation of a partnership.

In using these tactics to correct a partner's mistake, you should first determine whether or not the error can be corrected. In many players, the tendency to make certain bad bids is so deeply rooted that nothing short of death can eradicate it. For instance, there is the Mule. Due to his very nature it will be found impossible to make him give up rebidding his own hand. With such a partner all you can do is to recognize his mulishness and try to guess when it will crop out. When it does, pass, even though you know your hand calls for a bid. An example of this is the following. You hold

♠ x ♡ K Q J x x x x ◊ x x ♣ x x x

Your partner bids a spade, and you bid two hearts. He bids two spades. Of course it is now correct for you to bid three hearts. But suppose your partner is a Mule and that experience has taught you that he will never give up a hand. You know that if you bid three hearts, he will surely bid again and you will eventually land in a higher spade contract. In this situation, you must pass at two spades and probably take a small loss.

When playing with a Rabbit, you must take chances and overbid to counteract his timidity. With the Doubler, you have no protection whatsoever, but with many others, temperate reasoning at the right time should improve matters.

All that is necessary to say to the Leaper is: "I admire your leaping tactics very much, and I have noticed that you are very effective with many partners. However, your jumps leave me with a lot of guesses which I cannot handle. Why don't you bid a little more slowly with me? I promise not to pass your forcing bids under any circumstances, nor your non-forcing bids except with very good reason."

With a Notrumpist, suggestion will also bear fruit. First, you should compliment him on his play of notrump hands, and then point out that when you open the bidding, if he responds with a suit bid, instead of some number of notrump, subsequent bidding will be made much easier for you.

With the Steady Free Bidder or the Gallant Defender, just keep a record of the calamities you suffer with him. Show the record to him and tell him that while the penalties are perhaps justifiable, they are so upsetting and disturbing that they cause you to misplay other hands.

While you can correct certain idiosyncrasies of some partners, you can never correct all of them. Experience will show that every partner has his own style of bidding, and in order to get the best results it is necessary to vary your bidding methods and adapt them to your partner's. For instance, with a Gallant Defender as partner, you should be very careful about overcalling. With an Overbidder, you should try to hold a little in reserve; and with a Slamo-maniac, you should always underbid.

Another aspect that the winning Bridge player should consider is the calibre of play of his partner and his opponents. With a partner who is notoriously weak at Dummy play, care should be taken not to raise him to doubtful contracts, particularly when a Double may so upset him that he will lose several tricks more than he should. On the other hand, when your partner is a good Dummy player and your opponents are weak on defense, it is good policy to overbid slightly, relying on his skill to make the contract.

When your partner both bids and plays badly and your opponents are good players, you should do your best to end the rubber as quickly as possible and either to win or lose by small scores. After all, if your partner is so bad that you have but one chance in three of winning, what is to be gained by taking a set to keep the rubber alive when there is no assurance that he will not go down two thousand before the rubber ends; or why bid a Slam which he will probably misplay, when you can play the hand at game and get the rubber on the score sheet?

Conversely, with a fine partner and weak opponents, you can afford to take slight liberties. In this situation there is no hurry to end the rubber, and accordingly, you should try for any slam with a 50-50 chance of success, and should be slightly liberal in defending against a game bid by your opponents. However, even against weak opposition it does not pay to be reckless just because you think you have an advantage.

APPLIED PSYCHOLOGY

In order to use good psychology, first analyze your own game from an unprejudiced angle and discover your own idiosyncrasies with the intention of eliminating the objectionable ones; second, study the people with whom you play, and learn their peculiarities so that you can adapt your bidding and play to theirs; third, when you have a bad result, always take the blame yourself. It may be very soul-satisfying to wither your partner with a blast of invective but it doesn't add any points to your side of the ledger, and the fact that you may be absolutely right in your contention will do more to upset him than if you had been 100 percent wrong.

Cultivate the habit of analyzing swing hands as thoroughly as possible. If in a session of Bridge you are badly set at several game contracts, either remember the hands or write them down and study them later. You will probably find that your bidding was too optimistic. Conversely, if you missed a number of games, even though they could have been made only through favorable breaks, you will find that you were underbidding.

Remember that a player's game moves in cycles.

First there is the period of success. The overbidder finds that all finesses are right and that trumps always break. The underbidder misses games but suffers no loss, since his succeeding hands are even bigger. Nothing can go wrong, and instead of giving the credit to good fortune, the player attributes his success to his own genius. His peculiarities become exaggerated. The overbidder is at a Slam when he should be at game, or at game when he should have stopped at two; while the underbidder always has one or two tricks in reserve at whatever he contracts for.

Then things start to go wrong. The player enters a period of bad cards and bad breaks. The overbidder finds that he is not only bidding too much but that the opponents are doubling and punishing him severely. The underbidder

misses a vulnerable game and the next hand his opponents
go out with a Slam.

Rare indeed is the player who can say "Under the
bludgeonings of chance, my head is bloody but unbowed."
With the great majority, bad luck first warps their judgment and then causes them to lose confidence in themselves.
The overbidder tries to recoup his losses by desperate
chances. The underbidder crawls further and further into
his shell. But whatever the player's nature may be, he has
one remedy. When he finds he is going stale he should for-
get the game for a week or two. Then returning to it with
a new enthusiasm, he will find his confidence restored and
his judgment back to normal.

CHAPTER XXXVII

Duplicate Bridge

THE frequent playing of Duplicate Bridge is one of the best methods to improve one's game. Every player makes mistakes which are unnoticed or overlooked if made in rubber Bridge. But when they occur in Duplicate, they are laid bare by comparison with the scores made by others playing the same cards, and stand out in bold relief for all to see. When a player's score suffers by such comparison he naturally seeks to know the reason, and as the other players are only too glad to enlighten him he does not have to remain long in ignorance. Knowledge of the game learned in this way is not readily forgotten.

Duplicate, more than anything else, encourages extreme accuracy and precision in bidding and play. The slam-bang, leaping type of player may have fair success in a rubber game where his losses may in part be compensated for by the occasional big swings which he builds up. In Duplicate, with match-point scoring, however, a 10-point differential may be just as important as 2,000 points, and no hand is unimportant. For instance, consider the following hand, played in an eight-table Pair Duplicate game with match-point scoring:

North was dealer. North and South were vulnerable; East and West, not vulnerable:

score represents 30, 40 for an extra trick and a 50-point bonus for a partial score; while Pair Three, of course, went down two tricks, vulnerable. Pair Four bid and made two clubs to score 40 points and 50 for the partial score. Pair Five made two tricks over its one-notrump contract. Pair Six was set one trick; while against Pair Seven, the opponents got into the bidding and were doubled. Pair Eight bid and made exactly one notrump.

At either Duplicate or rubber Bridge the result obtained by Pair One was the best possible and was substantially better than that obtained by any of the other pairs. As under the match-point system of scoring one point is awarded for each pair defeated, Pair One received 7 match points. Pair Seven which was second best received 6 match points. Pair Five received 5 match points for having a better score than five other pairs, etc.

In order for North to make three notrump a tremendous amount of luck was required. Even in rubber Bridge we would consider the contract not only optimistic but very unsound. North's luck started with a heart opening by East giving him two tricks in that suit. It continued with a successful club finesse, adding four club tricks, and it held with a successful spade finesse netting two spade tricks, which with the diamond Ace produced nine. In spite of all this good fortune, an immediate shift to diamonds by either opponent upon securing the lead would probably have beaten the hand. However, three pairs did reach three notrump and the lucky pair received 7 match points, while the two that were set received, respectively, zero and one only; the three pairs that played the hand at one notrump were awarded 5, 4 and 2 match points respectively, a total of 11 as against a total of 8 given the three that contracted for game. The pair that played the hand at two clubs was just under average with three points; while Pair Seven was fortunate to have a chance to double a two-spade bid.

This hand brings out three important points for the Duplicate player to bear in mind. First, there is no point in bidding unsound games, because if you play a hand at a partial and are lucky enough to make sufficient tricks for game, you will nevertheless receive a good score. (Note Pair Five with its score of 5 points out of 7.) The second point is to be careful not to take a penalty of more than 100 points when the opponents have no game—Pair 15 bid two spades and went down 250 points to receive but one match point. The third point is to play hands at minor suits only when there is no other declaration at which to play them—Pair Four reached the fine contract of two clubs which cannot possibly be defeated, yet this pair received a below average score, due to the fact that Pairs One, Two and Five were lucky at notrump.

The third point is perhaps the most important to be drawn from this hand, and applies in an even greater measure to game contracts than to part scores. For example, while a hand may be perfectly safe at five clubs, in many instances it will also produce four notrump or four of a major suit, in which case the score you will receive for making five clubs will be very low. Experienced Duplicate players practically never play a hand at five clubs or five diamonds unless they hold 100 honors, or are prevented from playing notrump by the knowledge that the opponents hold a solid suit against them.

The mention of honors immediately brings us to another important point. Whereas, in rubber Bridge, honors may be practically ignored, in Duplicate, due to the match point gradation, they assume a tremendous significance, which frequently makes it profitable to play a hand at a poor suit in order to score honors. The following amusing example is a hand bid and played in the Men's Pair Championship of the American Bridge League in the summer of 1934.

South Dealer

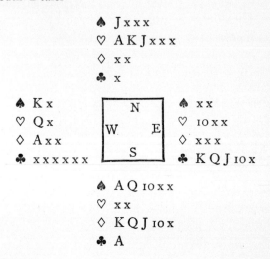

♠ J x x x
♡ A K J x x x
◇ x x
♣ x

♠ K x
♡ Q x
◇ A x x
♣ x x x x x x

N
W   E
S

♠ x x
♡ 10 x x
◇ x x x
♣ K Q J 10 x

♠ A Q 10 x x
♡ x x
◇ K Q J 10 x
♣ A

The Bidding:

South	West	North	East
1 ♠	Pass	2 ♡	Pass
3 ◇	Pass	4 ♠ ¹	Pass
5 ◇ ²	Pass	5 ♡ ³	Pass
6 ◇	Pass	Pass ⁴	Pass

¹ After South's strength-showing three-diamond bid, a Skip Level Shift, North was naturally strong enough to Jump to game.

² South now intends to bid a Slam but wants to play the hand at diamonds to score the honors, so bids five diamonds only.

³ North was slightly nervous, and bid five hearts, intending to pass if South bid five spades.

⁴ North realizes that South knows what he is doing and hence that his bid clearly indicated 100 honors. While North prefers spades he realizes that diamonds will probably be safe and passes in deference to South's judgment.

In the play of the hand, a club was opened and won by South's Ace. The King of diamonds was then led and West won with the Ace and returned the trump, whereupon declarer drew trumps and when the Queen of hearts fell on the second lead he was able to discard all of his spades except the Ace, making six diamonds, whereas the more logical contract of six spades would automatically have been defeated by the loss of a diamond and a spade trick.

Of course this hand could have been set at six diamonds if West had opened a heart and upon winning with the Ace of diamonds had led a second heart. This defense actually was employed against the one other team which bid the Slam in diamonds, but that team nevertheless obtained a good score, since practically all the others played the hand at six spades and were set one without honors.

Another example of the importance of honors is the following: North-South not vulnerable, East-West vulnerable, West deals and bids one spade, North passes, East bids three spades. South holds

♠ x x   ♥ x x x   ♦ A K Q J x x   ♣ A x

and bids four diamonds. West bids four spades, and North and East pass. In rubber Bridge, South would reason that this hand would be likely to take three tricks against the opponents' bid, and that if North could take one, they

would defeat four spades. Furthermore, he would visualize a certain set of three or four tricks at five diamonds,
and would pass. In Duplicate, South's reasoning would
take the following line: "Even though partner has a bust,
I will take seven tricks at diamonds and hence will be
penalized not more than 700 points, less 100 honors, a loss
of 600. Furthermore, I think the opponents can make four
spades, which will give them 120 points, plus the 500-
point bonus for game, or 620. Therefore, a 600-point loss,
will surely represent a saving of several match points."

The preceding hand brings us to competitive Duplicate
bidding and the "Howell Double." In Duplicate, a bonus
of 50 points is given for partial score. A pair bidding two
spades and making it scores 110. In this situation, a not
vulnerable opponent is very likely to overcall at three,
hoping to go down but two tricks for a loss of only 100
points, a resultant gain of several match points. Therefore, in these competitive situations the alert match-point
player frequently doubles when he would not consider doing so in rubber Bridge. The reasoning back of such a
Double is: "If the opponents can make three hearts, they
will obtain a very fine score even if undoubled, and if I
double them into game, it will add very few match points
to their score. On the other hand, in the event that their
bid was designed to prevent me from making two spades,
it behooves me to double. If we set them two tricks we shall
probably receive a top on the board."

Another interesting modification of match-point play
lies in the theory of overcalls. Whereas in rubber Bridge,
we must closely follow our Limit of Risk, in a match-point
game, it is frequently profitable to step out and take additional chances, since however large a penalty we incur,
we can do no worse than receive a zero score on one board.

Let us consider the following, in which we are Second Hand:

♠ K x x ♡ x x ◊ A Q 4 3 2 ♣ A x x

The Dealer bids one spade. In rubber Bridge, except in a partial-score situation, it would be very bad tactics to bid. It is very unlikely that our opponents can make game, and there is a good chance of our being substantially penalized. In a match-point game, however, we must take action, since otherwise our opponents will in all likelihood stop at a favorable partial-score contract, whereas if we bid, we, ourselves, may obtain a partial.

There are other instances in which defensive bidding may be varied in match-point play. Let us suppose that you are Third Hand, First and Second having passed, and hold six diamonds headed by the King-Queen-Jack and nothing else. In rubber Bridge, you would either pass or bid a semi-psychic one-diamond. In a match-point game, not vulnerable, you might endeavor to throw a bombshell at the opponents by an Opening bid of three diamonds, risking a substantial set. This nuisance bid would not be of any great help in rubber Bridge, since they would surely ignore the bid and contract for game. In a match-point game, however, it might easily prevent them from reaching the game declaration at which they would score the most points. For instance, they might score 620 at four spades, instead of 640 at three notrump, or 650 at four hearts, and while this 20- or 30-point saving in a rubber game would be negligible, it might represent a saving of many match points.

Finally, as our most important match-point modification, we come to the Fourth-Hand Opening bid. The reader will recall that in rubber Bridge, we recommended opening the bidding with a hand such as

♠ A K x x   ♡ x x x   ◇ A J x   ♣ x x x

in Third or Fourth position, in an effort to obtain a partial score. In Howell, where partial scores and 10-point differentials are so important, it is essential that we open the bidding any time we see a better than even chance of our side scoring points. For instance a hand such as

♠ A x x   ♡ A x x   ◇ x x x   ♣ K x x x

High card value 8.

which should be passed in a rubber game, should be bid one club if Fourth Hand in a Howell game.

Another form of Duplicate is the Team-of-Four game with total points. In this game, you and your partner play all the boards in one direction, while the other pair on your team play them in the reverse manner.

Here your problems are similar to those of rubber Bridge and, unlike the match-point game, 20- and 50-point differences mean practically nothing.

As the tactics of Team-of-Four Duplicate are quite similar to those of rubber Bridge, we feel that it furnishes the most desirable method of improving your game. All that is necessary is a group of eight players and a set of Duplicate boards. Comparisons may be made at the end of an evening's play not only of the large swings, but also of the small differences due to extra tricks, etc., and the player whose misplay or bidding error is responsible can learn to avoid its repetition in the future.

Glossary

In this book we have gone into a great many important phases of the bidding which have been completely omitted from other books on Bridge. It is necessary for us to use a great many terms, many of which will be new to our readers. Although the new and old terms are explained when first introduced in the text, we are grouping them here for ready reference.

Attacking Side. A general term used to designate the side which has opened the bidding.

Balanced Distribution. A distribution of 5-3-3-2, 4-4-3-2 or 4-3-3-3.

Bidder. The player who has opened the bidding.

Borderline Bid. A bid of one of a suit, made with a hand with a high card value of 7 to 9.

Business Double. A double made for the purpose of increasing the bonus received for setting your opponents.

Call. A bid, double, redouble or pass.

Chance. A response to an Opening bid of one in a suit, made with a weak hand, in order to give the original bidder an opportunity to show a very powerful hand.

Control-Showing Bid. A bid of a suit made to show either the Ace or a void.

Cue Bid. See Control-Showing Bid.

Defending Side. A general term used to designate the side whose opponents have opened the bidding.

Distribution. A general term applying to the division of the thirteen cards of a hand into suits.

Exploratory Bid. A bid made for the purpose of exploring game or Slam possibilities.

Forcing Bid. General term embracing all bids which we do not expect our partner to pass.

Free Bid. An immediate bid by Responder over Senior's overcall.

Free Double. There is no such thing.

Game Force. A forcing bid which requires that the bidding be continued to game.

High Card Value. The actual value of the honors held, expressed in points.

Informatory Double. See Takeout Double.

Invitational Bid. Any bid which strongly invites partner to continue.

Junior. The right-hand Opponent of the player who has opened the bidding.

Lead-Directing Bid. A bid made in order to show partner the correct lead.

Lead-Directing Double. A business double made to tell partner what suit to lead.

Level Shift. A bid of a second suit which permits partner to return to the first suit at the same level that the player making the Level Shift could have made a simple rebid.

Nominal Acceptance. An acceptance of a Slam Invitation which does not take the bidding past game.

Normal Limit of Risk. A penalty of two tricks vulnerable or three tricks not vulnerable.

One-Over-One. An Exploratory response at the range of one.

Penalty Double. See Business Double.

Penalty Pass. A pass of your partner's Takeout Double.

Playing Tricks. The number of tricks you expect to be able to take as declarer.

Positive Acceptance. An acceptance of a Slam Invitation which takes the bidding past game.

Pre-Emptive Bid. An Opening bid of three or four of a suit.

Principle of Anticipation. The proper selection of a bid or response, so that your partner's action will not leave you any new problems.

Principle of Limits. The first bid specifies certain limits. Subsequent bids define these more clearly.

Principle of Risk versus Gain. The possibilities of gain should more than compensate for the risk involved in any bid.

Qualified Game Force. A Game Force which partner may pass on very rare occasions.

Qualified Temporary Force. A Temporary Force which is qualified by the fact that the player making it has limited his hand by an original pass.

Responder. The partner of the player who has opened the bidding.

Responding Hand. The partner of the original bidder —Responder.

Rule of the Ace and the King. A scientific method devised to indicate when a hand warrants giving a Slam Invitation.

Rule of Return. In choosing between two suits bid by partner, return to the first suit unless you have a decided preference for the second.

Semi-Balanced Distribution. A distribution of 7-2-2-2, 6-3-2-2 or 5-4-2-2.

Senior. The left-hand opponent of the player who has opened the bidding.

Sign-Off. Any bid which strongly invites partner to pass.

Skip Level Shift. A bid of a second suit which does *not* permit partner to return to the first suit at the same level that the player making the Skip Level Shift could have made a simple rebid.

Slam Invitation. The first bid that directly suggests the Slam.

Slam Invitational Game Force. The immediate Jump response in a new suit.

Takeout Double. A double which you expect your partner to take out.

Temporary Force. A force which requires partner to respond once.

Trap Pass. A pass with a strong hand, made in the hope that the opponents will get into trouble.

Two-Bid. The Opening bid of two in a suit. It is forcing to game.

Unbalanced Distribution. A distribution including a singleton or a void.